Creative Groups Guide

Praise Under Pressure

13
Complete
Lessons

Adapted for Group Study by David Faust and Troy Jackson

STANDARD
PUBLISHING
Cincinnati, Ohio

Creative Groups Guide: Praise Under Pressure

By David Faust and Troy Jackson

Edited by Michael C. Mack

All Scripture quotations, unless otherwise indicated, are taken from the HOLY BIBLE, NEW INTERNATIONAL VERSION®. NIV®. Copyright © 1973, 1978, 1984 by International Bible Society. Used by permission of Zondervan Publishing House. All rights reserved.

Cover design by Listenberger Design Associates.

The Standard Publishing Company, Cincinnati, Ohio.
A division of Standex International Corporation.

03 02 01 00 99 98 97 96   5 4 3 2 1

ISBN 0-7847-0490-2

*C*ontents

oreword

Pressure. The very word can make us cringe.

To a quarterback, pressure is a three-hundred-pound lineman closing in for a crushing tackle.

To a young mother or dad, it's a sick baby crying at 3:00 A.M. for the fifth night in a row.

To a factory worker, it's an unreasonable boss who wants the job done twice as well in half the time.

To a busy executive, pressure means eighty-hour work weeks and a phone that never stops ringing.

To a teenager, it's peer pressure and never-ending schoolwork.

There's family pressure: "How should we handle our teenage son? How can we keep our marriage strong? How shall we care for our aging parents?"

Add to that some friendship pressure: "Why do I feel lonely even when I'm in a crowd of people? How can I find time just to laugh, listen, and pray with others?"

Above all, Christians experience faith pressure: "How can I stay close to the Lord when my life is busy and stressful? Where does God fit in all of this? How can I find time to pray?" Soul-stress may be the toughest pressure of all.

Fortunately, the Bible tells us about real people who faced the same problems we face today—people who managed to trust and obey God in a pressure-cooker world.

Tucked away in the middle of the Old Testament is the interesting historical account of David. David illustrates what it's like to serve God in a high-pressure world. He was no artificial hero, no religious smart aleck offering quick and easy answers to life's hard questions. His problems were genuine, but so were his prayers. Even in the midst of hardships, David came to God with heartfelt praise and honest questions. Through all the ups and downs of his life, David offered God praise under pressure.

This is a book about David's life and prayers. It's a book for broken people who dare to trust in the unbroken promises of God. It's a message of encouragement for people under pressure—for those who believe God holds the answer to life's puzzles, but who sometimes wonder exactly how all the pieces fit together. It's a book for people who want to follow Jesus, "the son of David."

Like David, we can learn to praise God—even when under pressure.

—David Faust, adapted from *Praise Under Pressure*

Introduction

Welcome to Creative Groups Guides!

Whether your group meets in a classroom at the church building or in the family room in someone's home, this guide will help you get the most out of your session.

You can use this Creative Groups Guide with or without *Praise Under Pressure,* the companion book written by David Faust. Use this guide even if you haven't read that book. But if you do read it, you'll be even more equipped for leading the group.

Each section in this guide includes two plans—one for classes and one for small groups. This gives the leader several options:

• Use the plan just as it is written. If you teach an adult Sunday school or an elective class, use Plan One. If you lead a small group, use Plan Two.

• Perhaps you teach a Sunday school class that prefers a small group style of teaching. Use the discussion questions and activities in Plan Two, but don't overlook the great ideas presented in Plan One. Mix and match the two plans to suit your class.

• Use the best of both plans. Perhaps you could start off your class with a discussion activity in Plan Two, and then use the Bible-study section in Plan One. Use the accountability, worship, or memory verse options presented in Plan Two in your Sunday school class. Use some of the "Sunday school" activities and resource sheets presented in Plan One in your small group meeting. Variety is the spice of life!

Resource sheets in each session are available for you to tear out and photocopy for your class or group. Overhead transparency masters are also included for most sessions. Use your own creativity as you decide how to make these resources work for you.

This guide has been developed to help you do several things. First, you'll be able to facilitate active and interactive learning. These methods help students remember and put into practice what they learn. Second, you'll help your class or group apply the lessons to their lives. These sessions will help your group members actually do something with what they're studying. Third, we've given you lots of options. Only you know what will work best in your class or group. Finally, support and encouragement are integrated into each session. Learning and application happen best when participants are helping one another. That may mean accountability if your group has built up the trust and caring it takes, or it may simply mean that people are lovingly encouraging one another to continue growing in knowledge and action.

How to Use This Guide

Each session begins with an excerpt from *Praise Under Pressure*. This excerpt summarizes the session at a glance. Use it in your preparation or read it to your class or group as an introduction to a session. The central theme and lesson aims help you understand the main ideas being presented and what outcomes you are looking for.

Materials you might need on hand to conduct your session are listed on the first page of each of the plans.

In both plans, there are three main parts to each session: Building Community, a warm-up activity or icebreaker question; Considering Scripture, Bible-study activities and discussion; and Taking the Next Step, activities or discussion that will help participants apply what they have learned.

In Plan One for classes, the names of activities are listed in the margins, along with the suggested time for each one. Use these as you plan your lesson and as you teach to stay on track. In most cases, optional activities are listed. Use these instead of or in addition to other activities as time allows.

A number of options are included in Plan Two for groups. Use the accountability-partner option to help the group support, encourage, and hold one another accountable. This works particularly well in a group in which trust has already been gained between participants. Accountability partners can help one another put what they are learning each week into practice. They can pray with and for each other throughout the week. They can "spur one another on toward love and good deeds" (Hebrews 10:24).

Other options include worship ideas and a memory verse. Use these at your discretion to help your group grow in love, devotion, and praise for God and for hiding his Word in their hearts.

Use this guide to help you prepare, but we suggest that you do not take this book to your class or group meeting and merely read from it. Instead, take notes on a separate sheet of paper and use that as you lead your group.

As a teacher or facilitator you know the pressure of preparing for and then leading a class or group. This Creative Groups Guide has been prepared to help you lead creative, fruit-bearing sessions without much pressure. But as you prepare and as you lead, remember yourself to give God praise under pressure!

One

Pressure Tested: How God Prepares a Leader

Our heavenly Father believes in preparation. He waited for centuries until "the time had fully come" before sending his Son Jesus to earth (Galatians 4:4). Then John the Baptist came as a forerunner to "prepare the way for the Lord" (Mark 1:2–4). After Jesus began his public ministry, he spent three years teaching his twelve apostles by word and example, preparing them for service.

Do you ever wonder what the Lord has been doing to prepare *you* for service? How does God prepare a leader, anyway? Nothing is wasted in God's economy. Our childhood experiences, our hurts, practical skills we develop, wise teachers and advisers we encounter along the way, lessons learned in the school of hard knocks—all play a part in preparing us for useful service.

David eventually became one of the greatest leaders of all time. But first he had to be "pressure-tested."

—David Faust, *Praise Under Pressure*

Central Theme	God can use life's pressures and problems to deepen our character and prepare us for effective service.
Lesson Aim	Participants will learn how David was prepared to serve God, and they will consider how their own past experiences have equipped them for effective ministry to God and others.
Bible Background	1 Samuel 16; Psalm 139
For Further Study	Read the Introduction and Chapter 1 in *Praise Under Pressure*.

Classes

BUILDING COMMUNITY

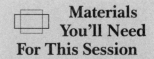 Distribute copies of <u>Resource Sheet 1A</u>. It contains a checklist that will help students reflect on the importance of preparation and on the ways God has prepared them for service. Point out that **it's always good to be prepared, and our confidence increases when we know we are well-prepared for a task.**

Ask your class to form groups of four to six, take a minute or two to fill in the chart, then discuss their answers with the rest of the group.

After about five minutes, say, **It's encouraging to realize that God uses our life experiences to prepare us for service in his kingdom. In our study today we're going to see how God prepared David to become a great leader, and we'll see how our own past experiences have equipped us to serve God and others.**

Write the words PREPARED and UNPREPARED on the chalkboard before class members arrive. When class begins, ask the group to call out a word or two to finish each of the following sentences. Write their answers on the chalkboard.

PREPARED:

1. During the past week, one task I have prepared for is . . .

2. When I am fully prepared for a task, I feel . . .

UNPREPARED:

1. One area of life where many people are poorly prepared is . . .

2. When I am unprepared for a task, I feel . . .

Lead into the Bible study by saying, **Today we're going to see how God prepared David for his task of leading the nation of Israel. In the process, we can also examine our own lives to see how the Lord has prepared each of us for effective service.**

CONSIDERING SCRIPTURE

Explain that this study of *Praise Under Pressure* is based on the life of David (as recorded in 1 and 2 Samuel) and the Psalms that David wrote.

Getting Prepared
8 Minutes

> **Materials You'll Need For This Session**
>
> Chalk and a chalkboard, copies of Resource Sheets 1A–1C, pencils or pens, an overhead projector and Transparency 1A

OPTION
Complete the Sentences
8 Minutes

Large Group Discussion and Mini-Lecture
20–25 Minutes

Ask the class, **What do you know about King David? What words come to mind to describe him?**

Allow them to respond briefly, and then ask volunteers to read the Scripture passages listed on <u>Resource Sheet 1B</u>. Use the questions to stimulate discussion.

As a concluding summary for the Bible study, display <u>Transparency 1A</u>. It lists five ways David was prepared for service. Use the following quotes from *Praise Under Pressure* to comment on each point.

1. God gave David a FAITHFUL FAMILY.
David grew up within a rich heritage of faith that stretched back several generations. It wasn't by chance that he grew up in Bethlehem. His great-grandmother was Ruth, whose story of faith appears in the Old Testament book that bears her name. . . . Eventually Ruth married Boaz, a landowner and leader in Bethlehem. No one paid much attention as these two newlyweds settled into their rustic life together, but "big doors turn on little hinges." Something big "clicked" in the plan of God as Ruth and Boaz passed along a heritage of faith to their son Obed and then to their grandson Jesse (who was the father of David).

Many years later, Jesus Christ was born there in Bethlehem (the "City of David"). In terms of his human genealogy, the Son of God was descended from the lineage of Ruth and Jesse and David (Matthew 1:5, 6). Never underestimate the influence of a faithful family!

2. God saw in David a COMMITTED HEART.
When Samuel arrived in Bethlehem, he invited Jesse and his sons to join him in offering a sacrifice to God. The oldest son, Eliab, was an impressive looking fellow. Samuel sized him up and thought, "Surely the Lord's anointed stands here before the Lord" (1 Samuel 16:6).

First impressions are not always correct, however. Eliab might have been man's pick, but he was not God's. . . .

Don't misunderstand. Outward beauty is not *wrong*. It just isn't *enough*. David himself was a nice looking man. He was "ruddy" (that is, he probably had auburn or reddish hair and possibly a fair or reddish complexion, "with a fine appearance and handsome features" (1 Samuel 16:12). But the Lord was more interested in the condition of his heart than with the curl of his hair or the breadth of his shoulders.

3. God taught David discipline through HUMBLE SERVICE.
David learned *patience*. Herding sheep takes time; so does leading people. . . .

He learned *responsibility*. . . . Why should God let David lead his nation if he can't even handle a flock of sheep? It's important to honor God in the small tasks. Get up in the morning and go to work. Go to class. Pay the bills. Be faithful in the small things. God prepares us to reach our long-term goals through the "ordinaries" of everyday tasks.

He learned *quietness*. David's obscure years with the sheep were not wasted. They provided time for uninterrupted prayer and communion with God. . . .

He learned *humility*. In God's order of things, "humility comes before honor" (Proverbs 18:12). David wasn't born a powerful king; he was the eighth son of a humble shepherd. While his brothers auditioned before Samuel, David toiled away on some obscure hillside, outside the spotlight of public view. This was all part of his pressure testing.

4. God refined David's GIFTS AND TALENTS

David possessed an unusual combination of skills. He was tough—a courageous warrior in a time of violent hand-to-hand combat. He also was thoughtful and sensitive—a writer of prayers and songs. He was an outdoorsman who could survive alone in the wilderness, but he also was an inspiring leader of men and a good public speaker. Perhaps his most surprising skill was his capability as a musician.

5. God strengthened David through THE SPIRIT'S PRESENCE AND POWER.

In the end, David's success as a leader did not depend on his looks, his physical strength, his musical skill, or any of his other talents. The key was the presence and power of God.

As a sign of God's call to service, Samuel took a horn of oil and anointed David in the presence of his brothers, "and from that day on the Spirit of the Lord came upon David in power" (1 Samuel 16:13). Even others who met David recognized "the Lord is with him" (1 Samuel 16:18).

Distribute a copy of Resource Sheet 1B to each member of the class. Divide the class into five small groups, and assign each group one of the questions listed on the resource sheet.

Ask each group to read the Scripture and discuss their question. After five minutes, ask each group to report its findings briefly to the entire class.

Display Transparency 1A and present a mini-lecture based on each point, using quotes from *Praise Under Pressure* provided above.

OPTION
Small Group Discussion and Mini-Lecture
20–25 Minutes

Personal Preparation Inventory
10–12 Minutes

TAKING THE NEXT STEP

Provide each member of the class with a copy of <u>Resource Sheet 1C</u>. Be sure each person has a pen or pencil.

Allow two or three minutes for each person to fill out the sheet, and then divide the class into groups of three or four people. Each person should share his or her answers with the other members of the group. The class session can conclude by having group members pray for one another.

OPTION
One Way Sharing
10–12 Minutes

Divide the class into groups of three or four people each. Each person should complete the following statements:

1. One way my past is like David's is . . .
2. One way my past is different from David's is . . .
3. One way I need to prepare myself to serve God is . . .

Each group then concludes with prayer.

Groups

BUILDING COMMUNITY

1. Explain that the *Praise Under Pressure* series will focus on the life of David and the Psalms. Brainstorm with the group: **How do you feel about David? What do you know about him? What were his strengths and weaknesses?** (See the Introductory chapter of *Praise Under Pressure* for ideas.)

2. OPTION: Ask each member of the group to tell about something he or she has done that required a lot of preparation. (For example: passing a difficult test, running a mini-marathon, preparing a meal for a large group.)

3. OPTION: Ask each person to tell the group about a time when he or she felt unprepared for an important event or task.

4. OPTION: Ask each person to respond to this question: **What is the hardest part of preparing to face a new day?** (For example: getting out of bed in the morning, driving in rush-hour traffic, facing an unpleasant task at work, getting children off to school.)

CONSIDERING SCRIPTURE

Read Psalm 139:13–16.

1. Based on these verses, how would you describe God's involvement in David's life?
   a. Curious bystander
   b. Aloof general
   c. Caring craftsman
   d. Other: _____

2. How would you describe God's current involvement in your life?
   a. Curious bystander
   b. Aloof general
   c. Caring craftsman
   d. Other: _____

Materials You'll Need For This Session

Bibles, pens or pencils, note cards, Resource Sheet 1C

Accountability Partners
When partners meet,
have them share their
completions of these
statements: (1) When I
think about my past,
what I'm most grateful
for is . . . (2) When I
think about my past,
what bothers me most
is . . . (3) When I think
about my future service
to God, what I feel best
prepared for is . . .

OPTION
Worship Ideas
Focus your worship on
God's familiarity with
"all our ways." Ask mem-
bers to write on a note
card a brief prayer para-
phrased from Psalm 139.
Prayers can focus on the
Lord's *knowledge* of our
daily activities (vv. 1–6),
his constant *presence* in
our lives (vv. 7–12), and
his *concern* for our
anxious thoughts
(vv. 23, 24). Allow sev-
eral volunteers to read
their prayers while the
group bows together.

OPTION
Memory Verse
"Search me, O God,
and know my heart; test
me and know my
anxious thoughts. See
if there is any offensive
way in me, and lead me
in the way everlasting"
(Psalm 139:23, 24).

Read 1 Samuel 16:1–13.

3. The Lord sent Samuel to anoint one of Jesse's sons as king. Why didn't the Lord let Samuel know in advance which of the sons was the chosen one?

4. Why did Samuel at first believe Eliab was the one God had chosen?

5. What does it mean to say, "the Lord looks at the heart" (1 Samuel 16:7)?

6. Whom have you overlooked because of outward appearances and first impressions?

7. What specific qualities do you see in David's life which equipped him for effective service to God? (See also 1 Samuel 16:18.)

TAKING THE NEXT STEP

1. Give each group member a copy of <u>Resource Sheet 1C</u>. Provide each person with a pen or pencil. Have members fill out the Personal Preparation Inventory and then share their answers with the group. (You may prefer to move into groups no larger than three or four people for this activity.)

2. OPTION: Each person should complete the following statements:
   1. One way my past is like David's is . . .
   2. One way my past is different from David's is . . .
   3. One way I need to prepare myself to serve God is . . .

Are You Prepared?

*Check **one** item in each of the categories below.*

A. I would feel *well-prepared* if God asked me to:

___ Teach a lesson to a group of three year olds
___ Build a house
___ Sing a solo in front of a large audience
___ Paint a picture
___ Serve as a missionary in South America
___ Bake a pie
___ Run a 3.1 mile cross-country race
___ Write a poem
___ Prepare and serve a meal for a large group
___ Visit a sick person in a hospital
___ Handle financial records for an accounting firm
___ Other: _____

B. I would feel *totally unprepared* if God asked me to:

___ Teach a lesson to a group of three year olds
___ Build a house
___ Sing a solo in front of a large audience
___ Paint a picture
___ Serve as a missionary in South America
___ Bake a pie
___ Run a 3.1 mile cross-country race
___ Write a poem
___ Prepare and serve a meal for a large group
___ Visit a sick person in a hospital
___ Handle financial records for an accounting firm
___ Other: _____

Reflection Questions

1. Read Psalm 139:13–18. According to these verses, when did God become actively involved in David's life?

2. Read 1 Samuel 16:1–6. Why did Samuel at first believe Eliab was the one God had chosen as the next king of Israel?

3. Read 1 Samuel 16:7. What are the things people look at? What are the things the Lord looks at?

4. Read 1 Samuel 16:8–11. Why do you think Jesse failed to invite his youngest son David to the sacrifice?

5. Read 1 Samuel 16:12, 13, 18–23. What specific qualities do you see in David's life that equipped him for effective service?

Personal Preparation Inventory

PART ONE: Circle any of the following experiences which have made you the person you are today. Following those you have circled, indicate whether these experiences have equipped you to serve God more effectively.

	DEFINITELY	PERHAPS	NOT AT ALL
A. Healthy family that taught me to love God	_____	_____	_____
B. Family problems I had to overcome	_____	_____	_____
C. My experiences in school or college	_____	_____	_____
D. A job I disliked, but had to do	_____	_____	_____
E. A job I loved, which helped me develop an important skill	_____	_____	_____
F. Time with an influential person who served as a role model	_____	_____	_____
G. A time when I learned "the hard way" the importance of being humble	_____	_____	_____
H. A time when I became more aware of God's presence in my life	_____	_____	_____
I. Other: _____	_____	_____	_____

PART TWO:

I think God is preparing me for _____

_____

To be better prepared to be useful to God, the next step I need to take is _____

_____

Pressure Tested
FIVE WAYS DAVID WAS PREPARED FOR SERVICE

1. God gave David a FAITHFUL FAMILY.

His heritage of faith:
- Rahab (Joshua 6:25; Matthew 1:5)
- Ruth and Boaz (Ruth 4:21, 22)
- Jesse of Bethlehem (1 Samuel 16:1; Matthew 1:6)

2. God saw in David a COMMITTED HEART.

"Man looks at the outward appearance, but the Lord looks at the heart" (1 Samuel 16:7; see 1 Samuel 13:14 and Psalm 139:23, 24).

3. God taught David discipline through HUMBLE SERVICE.

David, the youngest of Jesse's sons, learned valuable lessons as he tended his father's sheep.
- a. Patience
- b. Responsibility
- c. Quietness
- d. Humility

4. God refined David's GIFTS AND TALENTS.

By the time David entered the service of King Saul, he was a skilled *harpist, warrior, and public speaker* (1 Samuel 16:18).

5. God strengthened David through THE SPIRIT'S PRESENCE AND POWER.

"The Spirit of the Lord came upon David in power" (1 Samuel 16:13; see also 16:18 and Psalm 139:1–3).

Two

Overcoming Giant Problems

We all face some giant problems. That's why we need to look again at the familiar Bible story about David and Goliath. It's one of the best-known battles ever fought—a life-and-death struggle between a young man and a mighty giant whose very name, "Goliath," has become a synonym for something enormous and intimidating. On the surface, it's a gripping story even children can appreciate—a story of bravery and adventure, of good versus evil, of the weak overcoming the strong. From a historical perspective, it reveals important developments in the ongoing military struggles between Israel and their enemies, and helps explain David's rise to prominence.

But this is far more than a drab piece of history or a story for kids. From David's adventure, we can learn how to conquer our own giant problems.

—David Faust, *Praise Under Pressure*

Central Theme   For Christians, problems and challenges come with the territory. With a strong faith in God, we can emerge from any situation rejoicing in God's deliverance.

Lesson Aim   Participants will learn to handle giant problems by recognizing the enemy, refusing to be discouraged, remembering past triumphs, rejecting inadequate solutions, and rejoicing in God's victory.

Bible Background   1 Samuel 17; Psalm 20

For Further Study   Read Chapter 2 in *Praise Under Pressure*.

PLAN ONE lasses

BUILDING COMMUNITY

When the participants arrive, have them stand in a circle in the center of the room. Have each student, with each hand, take the hand of another participant. Each person must be holding hands with two different people. You cannot take the hand of a person standing next to you. After everyone is holding hands with two different people, instruct the participants, **Without letting go of either hand you are holding, attempt to untangle your arms so you form a complete circle. You have five minutes.** After five minutes, have the participants end their activity and take a seat. Whether they were successful or not, have participants share their reactions to the exercise.

Lead into the Scripture study by saying, **Whether trying to untangle arms as a group or trying to overcome physical illnesses, depression, financial difficulties, or frustration, life is filled with problems. How we handle the problems we face says a lot about who we are and on whom we depend in life's most trying times.**

Have participants think back to their earliest impressions of the story of David and Goliath from when they were children. Have people share those impressions with the group.

CONSIDERING SCRIPTURE

Have volunteers read *1 Samuel 17*. Display <u>Transparency 2A</u>, which contains several insights from *Praise Under Pressure*. Point out that **the way David responded to Goliath is a good model for how we can respond to difficulties in our own lives**. Go through each point, using the quotes by David Faust from *Praise Under Pressure* to flesh out each comment.

1. **Recognize the Enemy.**
   Goliath was physically powerful. He stood over nine feet tall (1 Samuel 17:4). . . . Goliath also was verbally abusive. . . . Defiantly Goliath taunted the Israelites: "Choose a man and have him come down to me. If he is able to fight and kill me, we will become your subjects; but if I overcome him and kill him, you will become our subjects and serve us"

The Human Knot
8 Minutes

**Materials
You'll Need
For This Session**

Resource Sheets 2A and 2B, Transparency 2A, pens or pencils

OPTION
Memories
8 Minutes

Mini-Lecture
25–30 Minutes

(1 Samuel 17:8, 9). . . . Goliath created an atmosphere of fear and intimidation. "On hearing the Philistine's words, Saul and all the Israelites were dismayed and terrified" (1 Samuel 17:11). . . . Another important point to notice about Goliath is his persistence. "For forty days the Philistine came forward every morning and evening" (1 Samuel 17:16). . . .

We can become so preoccupied with surface-level irritations (rainy weather, personality conflicts, cars that need repair, annoying co-workers) that we fail to recognize the real enemy behind our giant problems. "For our struggle is not against flesh and blood, but . . . against the spiritual forces of evil in the heavenly realms" (Ephesians 6:12). Our enemy the devil is like a roaring lion seeking someone to devour (1 Peter 5:8).

2. Refuse to Be Discouraged.

Discouragement reigned, and the more David spoke about fighting the Philistine, the more others tried to discourage him. . . . Any time you undertake a noble act of faith, there will be people who try to discourage you. . . . To overcome giant problems, we must refuse to accept the gloomy predictions of the skeptics who question our motives and who have no faith in the power of God.

3. Remember Past Triumphs.

David was no stranger to danger. He made his case to King Saul: "Your servant has killed both the lion and the bear. . . . The Lord who delivered me from the paw of the lion and the paw of the bear will deliver me from the hand of this Philistine" (1 Samuel 17:36, 37).

Past victories can give us confidence to fight today's battles. Smaller triumphs can help us face big battles with boldness and confidence. . . . God has helped us in the past. He will help us with the giant problems we face today.

4. Reject Inadequate Solutions.

Trying to be helpful, Saul put some of his own special battle gear on David to prepare him for combat: a tunic, a coat of armor, and a bronze helmet. . . . Finally he [David] told King Saul, "I cannot go in these, . . . because I am not used to them." If David was going to defeat the giant, he had to be himself! He had to go with his own God-given strengths (1 Samuel 17:39).

Instead, David chose to face the giant with simpler tools: his shepherd's staff, five smooth stones, and a leather sling (1 Samuel 17:40).

When we're faced with the world's inadequate solutions, we must choose God's way—the way of faith.

5. Rejoice in God's Victory.

It wasn't David's skill that won the battle that day; it was God's power. It wasn't a smooth stone that made the difference; it was a strong faith.

Perhaps David looked back on this great victory when he wrote Psalm 20:6–8: "Now I know that the Lord saves his anointed; he answers him from his holy heaven with the saving power of his right hand. Some trust in chariots and some in horses, but we trust in the name of the Lord our God. They are brought to their knees and fall, but we rise up and stand firm."

Goliath posed quite a problem for the people of Israel. He was vastly superior physically to anyone in Israel's camp. The majority of Israel responded to the challenge differently than David did. Have volunteers read *1 Samuel 17*. Distribute copies of <u>Resource Sheet 2A</u>. Have students work on the worksheet for fifteen minutes contrasting the way David responded to Goliath with the way the rest of the army did. After they are done, have the class come back together to share their findings.

OPTION
Contrasting
25–30 Minutes

TAKING THE NEXT STEP

Have participants break into groups of four. Pass out copies of <u>Resource Sheet 2B</u>. This worksheet has three questions to help class members confront problems in their own lives and begin to develop faith-driven responses.

Small Group Responses
10–15 Minutes

Churches are not without their share of challenges. If your church at present is facing an obstacle or a big transition (such as a large financial need or a staff transition), spend some time as a group answering the following question, **As our church faces <u>fill in the blank</u>, what can we as a congregation learn and apply based on how David responded to Goliath?**

OPTION
Take the Challenge
10 Minutes

PLAN TWO  **Groups**

BUILDING COMMUNITY

1. Have group members answer the following question: **When you were faced with a seemingly impossible math problem for homework in high school, how did you handle it?**

2. OPTION: Have participants share with the group their thoughts on the following question: **What do you think is the biggest problem facing our nation today?**

CONSIDERING SCRIPTURE

Read 1 Samuel 17:4–11.

1. If you saw a person over nine feet tall threatening you, what would be your first reaction?

2. How did King Saul and the Israelite army respond to Goliath?

Read 1 Samuel 17:17–37.

3. How did David respond when he first encountered Goliath?

4. Compare and contrast the ways David and the rest of the Israelite army faced the problem of Goliath.

5. When David let it be known that he was interested in fighting Goliath, how did others respond?

6. How had God prepared David for this battle with Goliath?

7. Why was David so confident as he prepared for battle?

Read 1 Samuel 17:38–50.

8. Why did David not use the armor provided by Saul?

9. As David walked toward Goliath to engage him in battle, what do you think was on David's mind?

Accountability Partners

Discuss with your partner one way you will apply the lessons learned from David's encounter with Goliath to a problem you are presently facing. Through a phone call or meeting, encourage one another to follow through on your action steps.

OPTION
Worship Ideas

Read together Psalm 20. Have each member share with the group the verse that best illustrates his or her present situation. Is this a time of distress, a time of anticipation, a time of victory, or a time of trust for you? After everyone has shared, spend some time in prayer, each person praying for the person on his or her left based on what he or she has shared.

OPTION
Memory Verse

"'The Lord who delivered me from the paw of the lion and the paw of the bear will deliver me from the hand of this Philistine.' Saul said to David, 'Go, and the Lord be with you'" (1 Samuel 17:37).

10. Imagine you've just read the story of David and Goliath for the very first time. Are you surprised at the outcome? Why or why not?

TAKING THE NEXT STEP

1. When you face difficult problems in your life, how do you respond?

2. Which person do you identify with the most in 1 Samuel 17?
   a. The Israelite army—afraid to take any steps at all
   b. Eliab (David's brother)—angry and critical
   c. David—filled with excited faith, ready to tackle big challenges
   d. Saul—happy when someone else is willing to try, but frightened to tackle a big challenge myself
   e. Goliath—lately I've been living as if I were self-reliant, an enemy of God

3. What problem or obstacle are you facing today?

4. What first step can you take to deal with your problem in a manner consistent with the example of David as he battled Goliath?

Fear or Faith?

Read 1 Samuel 17. As you read the passage, fill in the columns below in order to compare and contrast the approach of Saul and the Israelite army to Goliath with the approach of David to Goliath.

The Israelite Army's
Approach to Goliath

David's Approach to Goliath

Confronting Our Problems

With your group of four, share your answers to the following questions.

1. When you face difficult problems in your life, how do you respond?

2. What problem or obstacle are you presently facing?

3. What first step can you take to deal with your problem in a manner consistent with the example of David as he battled Goliath?

How To Handle GIANT Problems

1. Recognize the Enemy

2. Refuse to be Discouraged

3. Remember Past Triumphs

4. Reject Inadequate Solutions

5. Rejoice in God's Victory

Three

Target Practice: Coping With Angry People

Anger presents a difficult dilemma for Christians. How can you deal with your angry feelings and still be kind, gentle, Christlike, and self-controlled? How can you "be angry and sin not" (Ephesians 4:26)?

Even if you manage to keep your own anger under control, you still have to cope with the anger of others. Do you ever encounter hostile people who take out their frustrations on you? Do others try to make you the scapegoat for their anger, even when you've done nothing to harm them? How can you keep your cool when others try to use you for target practice?

As David struggled to offer God praise under pressure, he frequently faced hostile enemies. In particular, he became a target of the rage and temper tantrums of his angry employer, King Saul. David's story can help us cope with the angry people in our lives.

       —Adapted from David Faust, *Praise Under Pressure*

Central Theme   With God's help we can handle our own anger in a healthy way and respond with wisdom and grace to hostile people we encounter.

Lesson Aim   Group participants will gain a clearer understanding of the Bible's perspective on anger and develop a strategy for dealing constructively with people who make them a target for unhealthy expressions of anger.

Bible Background   1 Samuel 18, 19; Psalm 55

For Further Study   Read Chapter 3 in *Praise Under Pressure*.

Classes

BUILDING COMMUNITY

Divide the class into groups of two. Provide each group of two students with a small section of a recent newspaper (include the sports page and articles on world, national, or local news). Provide each group a pair of scissors. Ask them to find and cut out any news item, editorial, or other article that describes a situation involving anger.

After about five minutes, ask each group to pin its clipping on the bulletin board and briefly explain how the articles portray the problem of anger.

Before class, write the following statements on the chalkboard:

Most of the time, anger causes more problems than it solves. People today are angrier than they used to be.

Ask members of the class to raise their hands if they agree with each statement. Ask them to explain, in a sentence or two, why they feel this way. Then ask those who disagree to do the same.

CONSIDERING SCRIPTURE

Lead into the Bible study by saying, **The word *anger* is just one letter short of *danger*. For many people, coping with anger is a tough battle. But in one short verse, Ephesians 4:26, the Bible offers a well-balanced approach to dealing with anger.**

To those who suppress and deny anger, the message is, "Be angry." Stop deceiving yourself by pretending you have no anger. Anger itself is not wrong. God himself expresses wrath or righteous indignation against evil, and Jesus demonstrated holy anger when faced with stubborn, unrepentant sin (see Romans 1:18, Mark 3:5).

On the other hand, to the hostile, rage-filled person who blows others away with fits of rage, the Bible says, "Sin not." Don't use your anger as a tool to hurt people or allow yourself to dishonor God by your loss of self-control. According to James 1:19, 20, all of us must learn to be "quick to listen, slow to speak and slow to become angry, for man's anger does not bring about the righteous life that God desires."

Newspaper Search
10–12 Minutes

OPTION
Agree-Disagree
5–7 Minutes

Mini-Lecture and Brainstorming
10–15 Minutes

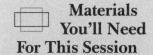 **Materials You'll Need For This Session**

Newspapers, several pairs of scissors, bulletin board, thumb tacks, chalkboard and chalk, pens or pencils, Resource Sheets 3A–3C, Transparency 3A

It's also important to distinguish between angry feelings (which are a natural human response to some violation or hurt) and hostile, out-of-control behaviors (which clearly cross the line into sin). The list of sinful deeds recorded in Galatians 5:19–21 includes "hatred, discord, jealousy," and "fits of rage"; and "those who live like this will not inherit the kingdom of God."

Distribute copies of <u>Resource Sheet 3A</u>. Make sure everyone has a pen or pencil. Ask class members to brainstorm about the two paradoxical commands found in Ephesians 4:26.

In the left column, have them write down some constructive ways we can "be angry." Ask, **When is it right to be angry? Are there times when it would dishonor God if we were *not* angry?** In the right column, students should list destructive ways anger causes harm to ourselves or others.

After about two minutes, ask for volunteers to read what they have written on each side of the chart.

Say, **Dealing with anger isn't easy! "Better a patient man than a warrior, a man who controls his temper than one who takes a city" (Proverbs 16:32). It's especially hard when we have to live and work around others who are hostile or angry all the time. As we continue our study of the life of David, let's take a look at how he handled himself when he became a target of King Saul's temper tantrums.**

OPTION
Scripture Search and Discussion
12–15 Minutes

Distribute copies of <u>Resource Sheet 3B</u>. Have volunteers read the Scripture verses listed. Lead a discussion of each point, using David Faust's ideas below, found in Chapter Three of *Praise Under Pressure*.

Causes of Saul's Unhealthy Anger

1. Jealousy (1 Samuel 18:8, 9)
[Saul] was unhappy to see someone else honored above him. He reasoned, "They have credited David with tens of thousands, . . . but me with only thousands"—in other words, "They are more impressed with him than they are with me." As a result, "from that time on Saul kept a jealous eye on David" (1 Samuel 18:8, 9). . . .

Christians need to learn that we're on the "same team" with other believers. Why not be happy when someone else enjoys the spotlight? Why not rejoice with others instead of secretly envying them?

2. Insecurity (1 Samuel 18:8)
Saul began to worry that David would take away his throne: "What more can he get but the kingdom?" (1 Samuel 18:8). . . .

All of us want to feel secure and significant, but we don't need to put others down to feel better about ourselves. We need to find our security and significance in Christ.

3. Spiritual Factors (1 Samuel 16:14; 18:10; 19:9)
   Even strong believers go through discouragement and "faith stress." But Saul's heart was filled with a dark despondency and discontentment. He brooded. He fretted. He plotted to get revenge. His mind became clouded and pessimistic; his moods frighteningly unpredictable. Spiritually, Saul was running on empty. And he was running scared.

Results of Saul's Unhealthy Anger
1. Emotional wounds (Psalm 55:12–14)
   Anyone who has experienced emotional suffering can identify with David's plight. Saul's angry behavior created an atmosphere of confusion and tension.

2. Physical violence (1 Samuel 18:10, 11; 19:9, 10)
   But for David, there was more at stake than simply getting his feelings hurt. His very life was in danger as he labored in the house of King Saul. More than once, Saul flew into such a rage that he took a spear in his hand and hurled it at David, trying to pin him against the wall. David narrowly escaped with his life, managing to elude the spear each time.

3. Family complications (1 Samuel 18:20, 21)
   Talk about a rough start to a marriage! The bride's manipulative, angry father was scheming up plots for the groom's death! Anger poisons the roots of many a family tree. Unresolved, it can rot relationships between in-laws, spouses, and children.

4. Long-lasting bitterness (1 Samuel 18:29)
   Like a pot simmering on a hot stove, Saul's unhealthy anger toward David stayed at a slow boil. Saul "remained his enemy the rest of his days" (1 Samuel 18:29).

Present <u>Transparency 3A</u> and sum up six positive ways we can respond to angry people, using the following ideas by David Faust from *Praise Under Pressure*:

OPTION
Turning Down the Heat
5–8 Minutes

1. Examine Yourself First.
   All Saul did was blame David. David took the healthier route: he examined his own motives. He opened his heart to God and admitted his own anguish and fears (Psalm 55:1–8).

2. Don't Give Up Too Soon.
   David was remarkably patient with Saul. He didn't pout, whine, and lash back. He did what he was supposed to do. He kept serving in the Israelite army and defending his nation against the Philistines.

3. When Possible, Confront the Offender.
Don't engage in backbiting and gossip. Jesus instructed us to seek reconciliation and to confront offenders directly and in person (Matthew 5:23–26; 18:15–17).

4. When Necessary, Enlist the Help of Friends.
Jonathan, one of Saul's sons, recognized David's innocence and tried to intervene. Although Saul eventually rejected Jonathan's pleas in David's behalf, at least David had a friend who understood his dilemma and tried to help (1 Samuel 19:1–7).

5. When Necessary, Remove Yourself From the Situation.
David was patient, but he wasn't foolish. When Saul threw his spears, David eluded them. . . . David wisely took action to protect himself from Saul's vicious attacks. For us, it might mean changing jobs, finding a different roommate in the college dorm, breaking off an unhealthy relationship, or firmly confronting someone.

6. Trust God.
David didn't face Saul's anger alone. He said, "But I call to God, and the Lord saves me" (Psalm 55:16).

OPTION
Scripture Reading and Discovery
12–15 Minutes

On one side of the chalkboard, write: *Why Was Saul Angry?* On the other side of the chalkboard, write: *What were the results of Saul's Anger?*

Ask a volunteer to read aloud *1 Samuel 18:5–16, 28–30; 19:1–17*. After the Scripture is read, ask volunteers to come forward and write on the chalkboard an answer to the questions based on what they discovered from the Scripture reading. Discuss their answers with the class, using ideas from *Praise Under Pressure* (see above). Use Transparency 3A to show positive ways we can respond to others' anger.

TAKING THE NEXT STEP

Anger Self-Analysis
6–8 Minutes

Provide each member of the class with a copy of Resource Sheet 3C. Allow two or three minutes for each person to fill out the sheet, and then divide the class into groups of three or four people. Each person should select and share *one* of her or his answers with the other members of the group.

As the class session concludes, members of the group can pray for one another, asking God to help us deal with anger in a way that honors him.

PLAN TWO

Groups

BUILDING COMMUNITY

1. What makes you angry? Why?

2. If someone cuts in front of your car on the highway, what do you do?

3. In *Praise Under Pressure*, the author suggests that people may be angrier today than in the past. Do you agree or disagree?

4. What do you see in your daily life that suggests people around you are struggling with anger?

CONSIDERING SCRIPTURE

Read 1 Samuel 18:5–16;, 18:28–30; 19:1–10.

1. How would you describe Saul's opinion of David? How did his view of David change as time passed?

2. Why was Saul so angry with David?

3. The success of others sometimes breeds contempt. How do you respond to the success and notoriety of friends and relatives?
   a. With heartfelt joy
   b. With an outward smile, but inner jealousy
   c. With anger and resentment
   d. With little emotion of any kind
   e. Other: _____

4. What is the difference between healthy jealousy (like the kind described in Exodus 20:5 and 2 Corinthians 11:2) and unhealthy jealousy (like that of Saul)?

5. Saul's anger resulted in several negative consequences for David. Which of these can you relate to personally?
   a. Emotional wounds
   b. Physical violence

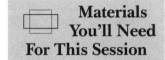

Materials You'll Need For This Session

Bibles, pens or pencils, Resource Sheet 3B

OPTION
Accountability Partners

Ask each other these questions: (1) What person or problem has caused you to be angry during the last week? (2) Did you deal with your anger in a way that was pleasing to God? (3) What is your greatest weakness in dealing with anger?

OPTION
Worship Ideas

Read Psalm 55:1–11, 16–23. Encourage group members to find phrases in this chapter that express the psalmist's concerns—how a believer feels while living in an angry world. Ask them also to find the psalmist's reasons to praise God. Express both the concerns and the praises to God in prayer, and include thanks to God for turning away his own anger from us because of the sacrifice of his Son Jesus Christ.

OPTION
Memory Verse

"Cast your cares on the Lord and he will sustain you; he will never let the righteous fall" (Psalm 55:22).

c. Family complications
d. Long-lasting bitterness
e. Other: _____

Read Psalm 55:12–14, 20, 21.

6. Why do you think Saul's actions were especially painful for David?

7. Think of a time when you were betrayed by a trusted friend. What emotions did you experience?

8. How do you usually deal with your own anger?
   a. I "stuff it" and hold it all inside
   b. I "fluff it," joke about it and act as if it's no big deal
   c. I "puff it," and express my anger openly and aggressively
   d. Other: _____

Read Psalm 55:22, 23.

9. How did David respond to Saul's anger?

10. Jesus encountered many angry people during his life and ministry. Does this fact encourage you? How?

TAKING THE NEXT STEP

1. What steps do you need to take to deal constructively with your own angry feelings? (You may wish to use Resource Sheet 3B, the "Anger Self-Analysis," and share one or more of your answers with the group.)

2. In *Praise Under Pressure*, the author suggests six steps to take in responding to the anger and frustration of others. (See Transparency 3A.) Which of these steps would help you the most right now?

"Be Angry . . . And Sin Not"

(Ephesians 4:26)

Constructive Uses of Anger   **Destructive Uses of Anger**

Saul: An Angry Man

CAUSES OF SAUL'S UNHEALTHY ANGER

1. Jealousy: 1 Samuel 18:8, 9

2. Insecurity: 1 Samuel 18:8

3. Spiritual factors: 1 Samuel 16:14; 18:10; 19:9

RESULTS OF SAUL'S UNHEALTHY ANGER

1. Emotional wounds: Psalm 55:12–14

2. Physical violence: 1 Samuel 18:10, 11; 19:9, 10

3. Family complications: 1 Samuel 18:20, 21

4. Long-lasting bitterness: 1 Samuel 18:29

Anger Self-Analysis

NEVER   SOMETIMES   OFTEN

1. Do I provoke others to anger?   ____   ____   ____

> *"An angry man stirs up dissension, and a hot-tempered one commits many sins"*
> *(Proverbs 29:22).*
> *"For as churning the milk produces butter, and as twisting the nose produces blood, so*
> *stirring up anger produces strife" (Proverbs 30:33).*

2. Do I practice patience and self-control?   ____   ____   ____

> *"Better a patient man than a warrior, a man who controls his temper than one who*
> *takes a city" (Proverbs 16:32).*
> *"A fool gives full vent to his anger, but a wise man keeps himself under control"*
> *(Proverbs 29:11).*

3. Am I petty, quick-tempered, or irritable?   ____   ____   ____

> *"Starting a quarrel is like breaching a dam; so drop the matter before a dispute breaks out"*
> *(Proverbs 17:14).*

4. Do I react to others' anger with
gentle, thoughtful words?   ____   ____   ____

> *"A gentle answer turns away wrath, but a harsh word stirs up anger. The tongue of the wise*
> *commends knowledge, but the mouth of the fool gushes folly" (Proverbs 15:1, 2).*

5. Do I listen to others' viewpoints
before reacting with anger?   ____   ____   ____

> *"My dear brothers, take note of this: Everyone should be quick to listen, slow to speak and*
> *slow to become angry, for man's anger does not bring about the righteous life that God*
> *desires" (James 1:19, 20).*

6. Do I meddle in conflicts
that others should resolve?   ____   ____   ____

> *"It is to a man's honor to avoid strife, but every fool is quick to quarrel" (Proverbs 20:3).*
> *"Like one who seizes a dog by the ears is a passer-by who meddles in a quarrel not his own"*
> *(Proverbs 26:17).*

TURNING DOWN THE HEAT

Here are six practical ways to respond to the angry people in our lives:

1. Examine Yourself First.

2. Don't Give Up Too Soon.

3. When Possible, Confront the Offender.

4. When Necessary, Enlist the Help of Friends.

5. When Necessary, Remove Yourself From the Situation.

6. Trust God.

Four

Friends in Need, Friends in Deed

*D*avid and Jonathan enjoyed one of the greatest friendships described in the Bible. On the surface, it's surprising these men would need friends at all. Both of them were rugged individualists—masculine, courageous warriors, unafraid to stand apart from the crowd. They first became acquainted after David killed Goliath. David's victory earned him widespread respect in Israel, but Jonathan was especially impressed. He and David were kindred spirits, and they soon developed a close bond (1 Samuel 18:1). Like all of us, they needed friends.

—David Faust, *Praise Under Pressure*

Central Theme — In the New Testament, we read, "Dear friends, let us love one another, for love comes from God" (1 John 4:7). One of the best ways we can love others is by working to build strong friendships with others.

Lesson Aim — This lesson will challenge participants to pay the price of true friendship, for God-centered friendships are immensely rewarding.

Bible Background — 1 Samuel 20; Psalm 133

For Further Study — Read Chapter 4 in *Praise Under Pressure*.

Classes

BUILDING COMMUNITY

Items needed include a VCR and a television set large enough for the class to see or a video projector and screen. The week before the class, tape a popular situation comedy or drama on television that often revolves around friendships. Possibilities include shows like *Seinfield*, *Friends*, and *ER*, or reruns of shows like *Cheers*, *The Andy Griffith Show*, or *The Mary Tyler Moore Show*. Select a three- to five-minute scene from the show that illustrates some aspect of friendship, whether positively or negatively. (Of course, you'll need to use great care with picking from some of today's shows. Be sure the scene you use does not cause anyone embarrassment or discord.) Show the scene to your class. Afterwards, spend about five minutes discussing the display of friendship portrayed on the television show.

Lead into the Scripture study by saying, **Unfortunately, Hollywood's portrayal of friendship rarely shows a complete picture of what friendship really involves. Friendship is more than just commonality. Friendship goes beyond doing what is easy. Friendships are only truly meaningful and rewarding when accompanied by hard work and commitment. This is the type of friendship that David and Jonathan shared.**

Have participants break into groups of four. Once in their groups, have them share with the other group members their answers to the question, **"Who was your first real friend and why?"** After several minutes of sharing, call the class back together and say, **Friendships are important and meaningful to us. Many of us can still remember with great detail the friends we had when we were quite young. David was no different. His friendship with Jonathan was one of the most meaningful and memorable relationships of his life.**

CONSIDERING SCRIPTURE

Have volunteers read *1 Samuel 20*. Have the class break into groups of four. Distribute copies of <u>Resource Sheet 4A</u>, which challenges participants to explore the need for friendship, the qualities of friendship, and the benefits of friendship.

TV Friends
8 Minutes

> **Materials You'll Need For This Session**
>
> VCR and television set, tape of TV show, Resource Sheets 4A and 4B, Transparency 4A, pens or pencils

OPTION
Sharing About Friends
8 Minutes

Group Discussion
30 Minutes

After twenty minutes, have the class come back together. Display Transparency 4A, which outlines the need, qualities, and benefits of friendships.

OPTION
Talk Show
25–30 Minutes

Have participants break into two groups. One of the groups should consist of about four to seven people. The other group should consist of all remaining class members. The group of four to seven people will be in charge of putting on a ten-minute talk show on friendship based on *1 Samuel 20.* The remaining class members will be the audience who will ask questions of the panel based on 1 Samuel 20. Once the groups are divided, pass out copies of Resource Sheet 4B to each group. After twenty minutes, have the group present its talk show for ten minutes.

TAKING THE NEXT STEP

Deepening Friendships
10–15 Minutes

A Sunday school class is often a great place to learn more about God and the Bible, but sometimes the environment makes it difficult to develop deep friendships with one another. Even if the class does a good job at developing friendships, there is always room for improvement. Spend some time brainstorming as a class in response to the question, **How can our class do a better job of developing a nurturing friendships like that of David and Jonathan?** After several suggestions have been offered, select one or two that are most feasible and exciting, and begin plans to actually make these changes or stage these events. To insure that the suggestions are enacted, have someone be in charge of the changes that are to occur.

OPTION
Christ-filled
Friendships
10 Minutes

Have participants break into groups of four. Say to the groups, **Sometimes even our deepest friendships fail to have a spiritual dimension. For some, one's relationship with Jesus Christ never enters into conversations, even when both friends are committed Christians. David and Jonathan's friendship certainly had a great deal of spiritual depth. As Jonathan said, they could, "go in peace" because their friendship was "in the name of the Lord" (1 Samuel 20:42). Spend the next several minutes sharing with your group some specific ways you will make Jesus a regular part of your conversations with one of your friends.**

Groups

BUILDING COMMUNITY

1. Have group members respond to the question, **Describe the person who was your best friend when you were twelve years old.**

2. OPTION: Have group members share their thoughts on the following question: **Compare and contrast the way television shows portrayed friendships in the sixties and seventies (on shows like *The Mary Tyler Moore Show*, *Happy Days*, and *Laverne & Shirley*) with the way television shows portray friendships today (on shows like *Seinfield*, *Cheers*, and *Friends*).**

CONSIDERING SCRIPTURE

Read 1 Samuel 18:1–4 and 1 Samuel 20.

1. How did Jonathan respond to David's accusation that his father Saul was trying to kill David?

2. Why did David believe he could confide in Jonathan even though he was making accusations about Jonathan's father?

3. Jonathan was put in the difficult position of deciding between two competing loyalties: family and friendship. By what criteria did Jonathan choose to help David and not his father?

4. Why did Jonathan develop such an elaborate plan to inform David of Saul's reaction to his absence at the King's table (vv. 18–23)?

5. What risks did Jonathan take for the sake of his friend David?

6. Why do you think Jonathan was willing to risk so much for David?

7. Are risks usually a part of what it means to be a friend? Why or why not?

OPTION
Accountability Partners
Discuss with your
partner ways that you
can be more open,
transparent, and real
with one another,
sharing what is really
going on in your lives so
real accountability and,
in a real sense, friend-
ship, can happen.

OPTION
Worship Ideas
Sing or read together
the hymn, *What a Friend
We Have in Jesus*. Then
have participants share
how Jesus is, in every
sense of the word, a
friend. Close the group
by having group mem-
bers thank God for all
their friends, and
especially Jesus.

OPTION
Memory Verse
"How good and pleasant
it is when brothers live
together in unity"
(Psalm 133:1).

8. What marks of true friendship do we find between David and Jonathan in this passage?

9. What made David and Jonathan such good friends?

TAKING THE NEXT STEP

1. What bonds you and your friends together?

2. To what lengths are you willing to go to help a close friend?

3. God is clearly at the center of the friendship between David and Jonathan. How can you make God more a part of your friendships?

What is a Friend?

Slowly reread 1 Samuel 18:1–4 and 1 Samuel 20 together as a group, noting in the appropriate columns any insights that we can learn about the need for friendships, the qualities of friendships, and the benefits of friendships.

Insights about Friendship
Learned from Jonathan and David

The Need for Friendships

The Qualities of Friendship

The Benefits of Friendship

It's Everyone's Favorite Afternoon Pastime...
The Samuel the Prophet Show!

Welcome to the exciting talk show of the day about 3,000 years ago, the *Samuel the Prophet Show*. Today's topic is friendship, and our very special guests include David son of Jesse, Jonathan son of Saul, and Saul son of Kish. As always, our host is Samuel!

GROUP A INSTRUCTIONS:

You are in charge of putting on a ten-minute talk show for the rest of the class on the topic of friendship. Begin by assigning the parts of Samuel (the host), Saul, David, and Jonathan. After parts are assigned, spend the next twenty minutes reading through 1 Samuel 18:1–4 and Samuel 20, noting the facts of the story and the nature of your particular character. Specifically look for marks of friendship between David and Jonathan. The rest of the class will be asking you questions about friendship based on this text. Be sure you know your character's part in the story well so you can respond to questions in a way consistent with the Scripture.

   Specific Instructions:
   • Samuel: Your job is to introduce the guests, field questions, and elicit responses. Be sure to keep the discussion moving and on the topic of friendship.
   • Saul: Your role is to describe the friendship of David and Jonathan from your perspective, which will obviously not be a favorable one.
   • David and Jonathan: Your roles are to share what it is like to be in such a life-changing friendship. Give us the insider's view of what real friendship is all about.

GROUP B INSTRUCTIONS:

You are the audience for today's *Samuel the Prophet Show*. Tickets are extremely hard to come by, so you are absolutely thrilled to be here and hope to actually get to ask a question of one of our guests. Spend the next twenty minutes carefully reading 1 Samuel 18:1–4 and 1 Samuel 20 together, jotting down creative questions one of you could ask either Saul, David, or Jonathan about the friendship Jonathan and David shared and the events recorded in this passage. Make sure the questions arise out of Scripture and relate in some way to the topic of friendship. Your goal as an audience is to try to understand why the friendship of David and Jonathan is so special. Try to make your questions serve that purpose. Be sure to ask questions of all three guests and to include as many audience members as possible by giving them a chance to ask a question.

Friendship Is . . .

(Marks of Friendship From *Praise Under Pressure*)
Based on 1 Samuel 20 and Psalm 133

1. **The Need for True Friends**

- · **Friends provide accountability**
- · **Friends provide encouragement**
- · **Friends help us grow**
- · **Friends make us more productive**

2. **The Qualities of True Friendship**

- · **Committed love**
- · **Shared resources**
- · **Consistent loyalty**
- · **Honest emotions**
- · **Spiritual depth**

3. **The Blessings of True Friendship**

- · **Unity in friendship is good and pleasant and honors God**
- · **Unity is pleasing to God and attractive to others**
- · **Friendships are truly a gift of God**

Five

Staying Sane in a Crazy World

*L*ife doesn't always make sense. . . . Sometimes even our *spiritual* lives don't make sense. Many believers go through times when life feels joyless; when spiritual clarity is replaced by confusion; when God's blessings seem to give way to the blues and the blahs.

It happened to David. Right when he was on the verge of greatness, his life turned upside down. David was fast becoming one of Israel's best-known warriors. But King Saul angrily set out to kill him. Instead of ruling from a throne, David was on the run. He was feeling desperate.

In one of the lowest moments of his life, David acted like a madman to escape capture and death. But he still managed to give God praise under pressure.

—David Faust, *Praise Under Pressure*

Central Theme	God deserves praise during stressful times, for even in our most desperate moments, he will comfort us, strengthen us, and faithfully meet our needs.
Lesson Aim	Participants will examine how they respond to pressure and develop practical ways to praise God and depend on him during times of stress.
Bible Background	1 Samuel 21; Psalm 34
For Further Study	Read Chapter 5 in *Praise Under Pressure*.

PLAN ONE

Classes

BUILDING COMMUNITY

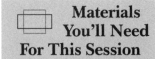

Before students arrive, write in big letters "STRESS" across the chalkboard, and along the left hand border of the board write the numbers one through ten. When the class convenes, say, **Together, let's create a top ten list identifying the ten leading sources of stress in our community/town/city.** After a top ten list has been created, lead into the Bible study by saying, **All of us have times when we feel pressured and stressed, anxious and worried, burdened and hassled. We are not alone. In today's passage, we see how David responded when life's pressures seemed unbearable.**

Several days in advance, ask two or three members of the class to create and present a short humorous skit portraying the way stress affects our lives.

CONSIDERING SCRIPTURE

Have a volunteer read *1 Samuel 21*. Divide the class into groups of four. Pass out copies of <u>Resource Sheet 5A</u>, which contains a number of discussion questions based on the passage. Allow the groups twenty minutes to work through the questions. Then reassemble the class, allowing a few minutes for the groups to share some of their findings with one another.

Have volunteers read *1 Samuel 21*. Then display <u>Transparency 5A</u>, revealing David's Top Five "Crazy-Making" Conditions. Use the quotes provided from *Praise Under Pressure* by David Faust to help explain each of these stressors that David encountered.

1. No Friends
Just days before, David said a tearful good-bye to his friend Jonathan (1 Samuel 20:41, 42). Problems grow more intense when we have to face them without the support of friends. "Pity the man who falls and has no one to help him up!" (Ecclesiastes 4:10).

Top Ten List
8 Minutes

> **Materials You'll Need For This Session**
>
> Chalk and chalkboard, Resource Sheets 5A, 5B, and Transparency 5A

OPTION
Mini-Drama
8 Minutes

Small Group Bible Study
20–25 Minutes

OPTION
Mini-Lecture
20–25 Minutes

2. No Food

Another problem was that David had nothing to eat. Weak and famished after days of hiding, he asked Ahimelech for bread or whatever else he could find (1 Samuel 21:3). Problems seem amplified when we're hungry, sick, or physically exhausted. David was desperate for food. How humbling it was for this great warrior to beg for bread!

3. No Sword

Not only was David hungry. He also was unarmed. He asked Ahimelech, "Don't you have a spear or a sword here?" (1 Samuel 21:8).

David must have been feeling desperate and vulnerable. Normally you might ask a priest for advice on spiritual matters, but you wouldn't ask a priest to arm you for battle! Ahimelech owned no arsenal of weapons. Ironically, though, the extra-large sword previously owned by the giant Goliath was wrapped in a cloth and hidden away somewhere in the tabernacle. Ahimelech offered David the huge weapon and said, "If you want it, take it; there is no sword here but that one." And David replied, "There is none like it; give it to me" (1 Samuel 21:9).

4. No Privacy

David faced yet another problem. He was no longer an unknown shepherd boy from the backwoods. Like today's celebrity who cannot go out in public without being swarmed by autograph seekers, David was now so well known that nearly everyone recognized his face. Just as Michael Jordan can't walk through a crowded Chicago street without someone noticing him, David the giant killer found it difficult to escape notice in Israel. There was no place to hide.

5. No Dignity

Now that Achish the king of Gath knew who he was, David grew even more afraid. What if Achish decided to kill him rather than risk the wrath of Israel's King Saul? Quickly David found a strange but effective solution to his predicament: he pretended to be insane. "So he pretended to be insane in their presence; and while he was in their hands he acted like a madman, making marks on the doors of the gate and letting saliva run down his beard" (1 Samuel 21:13).

What a humiliating scene! David, the great hero of faith, was acting like a raving lunatic. Even Achish seemed embarrassed. Sarcastically he said to his servants, "Look at the man! He is insane! Why bring him to me? Am I so short of madmen that you have to bring this fellow here to carry on like this in front of me? Must this man come into my house?" (1 Samuel 21:14, 15). If the situation weren't so serious, the king's words could sound humorous: one thing his city didn't need was a few more imported madmen!

But this incident certainly wasn't funny for David; and it's not funny to anyone who has ever tasted great mental or emotional distress. Crazy conditions can bring us to the breaking point.

TAKING THE NEXT STEP

Using the chalkboard, have the group make a list of the top 10 ways a Christian can respond to stress based on Psalm 34.

Have the class break into groups of four. Hand out <u>Resource Sheet 5B</u>. Have the groups work through "Good Times . . . Bad Times."

Top Ten List
10 Minutes

OPTION
"Good Times . . . Bad Times"
10 Minutes

roups

BUILDING COMMUNITY

1. When you were growing up, who was your strangest neighbor? Why?

2. OPTION: Give everyone a note card and a pen or pencil. Ask each person to write down one source of stress in your community/town/city, and then hand the card to the person on his or her right. Go around the group and let each person read what is on the cards.

CONSIDERING SCRIPTURE

Read 1 Samuel 21:1–9.

1. What stressful factors was David facing? List as many as you can.

2. Why did David flee to Gath?

3. David seems evasive in his answer to Ahimelech in verse 2. Why was he so careful?

4. Even in this awkward time, God provided for David. Cite some examples of God's provision to David.

Read 1 Samuel 21:10–15.

5. How do you think David felt when the people recognized him?

6. David was not afraid of Goliath, but he was fearful of Achish. Does this surprise you? Why or why not?

7. In the face of these pressures, why did David begin to act insane? Was his strategy effective?

Materials You'll Need For This Session

Bibles, note cards, pens or pencils, Resource Sheet 5B

OPTION
Accountability Partners
When accountability partners meet, have them share their responses to the following questions: (1) What has caused you to experience extra stress during the past week? (2) How can your partner help you and pray for you as you work through this issue?

OPTION
Worship Ideas
Focus your worship time on God's faithfulness in times of distress. Praise God for being present when we need him most. Thank God for ways he has aided you in times of stress in the past, and ask for strength to trust God even when you're under pressure.

OPTION
Memory Verse
"I will extol the Lord at all times; his praise will always be on my lips" (Psalm 34:1).

TAKING THE NEXT STEP

1. What circumstances in your life are "driving you crazy" right now?

Read Psalm 34.

2. What section of Psalm 34 is most encouraging to you? Why?

3. Give everyone a copy of <u>Resource Sheet 5B</u>, "Good Times . . . Bad Times." Discuss the questions one at a time.

Discussion Questions
1 Samuel 21

Read 1 Samuel 21:1–9.

1. What stressful factors was David facing? List as many as you can find.

2. David seems evasive in his answer to Ahimelech in verse 2. Why was he so careful?

3. Even in this awkward time, God provided for David. Cite some examples of God's provision to David.

Read verses 10–15.

4. How do you think David felt when the people of Gath recognized him?

5. David was not afraid of Goliath, but was fearful of Achish. Does this surprise you? Why or why not?

6. In the face of these pressures, why did David begin to act insane? Was his strategy effective?

Good Times . . . Bad Times

In your group, read through Psalm 34. Then respond to the following questions.

1. When do you find it most difficult to praise the Lord?

2. When do you find it easiest to praise the Lord?

3. Psalm 34:1 says, "I will extol the Lord at all times; his praise will always be on my lips." What one positive step do you need to take so this verse will ring true for you as well as David?

David's Top Five "Crazy-Making" Conditions

1. No Friends

2. No Food

3. No Sword

4. No Privacy

5. No Dignity

Six

Don't Cave In

*A*ccording to 1 Samuel 22:1, David fled to a cave in a place called Adullam. This cave . . . became David's unofficial headquarters while he was forced to hide from King Saul. David's gloomy surroundings in the cave almost seem fitting. He was down. He was in a pit. Saul's heart was as hard and unyielding as the cave's cold walls. . . .

Eventually, most of us spend time in the cave. (Maybe you're there right now.) We fall into pits of depression, caverns of grief, dark holes of doubt.

Sometimes it feels like we will never escape from the cave. But eventually we do; and in the process, God uses our spiritual spelunking to build our faith.

—David Faust, *Praise Under Pressure*

Central Theme	When people or circumstances confront us with change and insecurity and there is no place we can call home, we must keep our focus on God, trusting God to sustain us and deliver us.
Lesson Aim	Participants will learn that God is always present and in control. In fact, God often uses seemingly desperate times to teach us.
Bible Background	1 Samuel 22–26; Psalm 57
For Further Study	Read Chapter 6 in *Praise Under Pressure*.

Classes

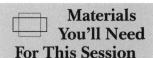

Materials You'll Need For This Session

Chalkboard; chalk; record, tape, or CD, and player; Resource Sheets 6A and 6B; Transparency 6A

BUILDING COMMUNITY

When participants arrive, pass out copies of <u>Resource Sheet 6A</u>. After about five minutes working on the handout, call the group together and have a few people share about the worst storms they have ever experienced. To lead into Bible study, say, **Whether we like it or not, we are often at the mercy of the weather, be it rain, snow, or extreme temperatures. Our hands can be tied also when it comes to the actions of other people. David was at the mercy of the most powerful man in Israel, King Saul, but David did not cave in under the pressure. Instead, he trusted God to sustain him and deliver him.**

Storm Stories
8 Minutes

Write the word *Moving* on the chalkboard. Have class participants share about a time when they moved. After several people have shared, say, **Few events are as unsettling as changing homes or places of residence. In today's study, we will see how David continued to trust God even as he spent several years with "no place to lay his head."**

OPTION
Word Association
8 Minutes

If space allows, play a game of musical chairs. After you have a winner, lead into Bible study by saying, **In Musical Chairs, you are always on the move, and are never sure if you will have a seat the next time the music stops. David spent several years on the move, fleeing from King Saul, rarely knowing where he would sleep at night. Yet, through it all, David trusted God to sustain and deliver him.**

OPTION
Musical Chairs
10 Minutes

CONSIDERING SCRIPTURE

Break the class into five groups. Assign each group a chapter of the Scripture (1 Samuel 22; 23; 24; 25; 26). Pass out <u>Resource Sheet 6B</u>, and have each group answer the questions according to its chapter. After twenty minutes, bring the groups back together and have each briefly share its findings.

Chapter Study in Groups
20–30 Minutes

Use <u>Transparency 6A</u>, "Finding Purpose in the Pits," to highlight how David was able to find purpose and even praise God during difficult times. Use the following quotes from David Faust in *Praise Under Pressure* to explain each point.

OPTION
Purpose in the Pits
30 Minutes

1. Attacked, But Not Alone

God provided David a new set of friends when he was in the cave. "All those who were in distress or in debt or discontented gathered around him, and he became their leader. About four hundred men were with him" (1 Samuel 22:2).

2. Victimized, But Not Vengeful

David was victimized but not vengeful. He confronted Saul with the truth, but not with violence or a spirit of revenge. David reasoned, *No matter what Saul has done to me, he's still God's anointed king. I have no right to take his life. If God wants him out of the way, I'll wait for God to take care of things in his own time.*

3. Angry, But Able to Accept Advice

Abigail was wise. She brought a large gift (enough bread, wine, meat, grain, and fruit to feed David's men), and she brought a peacemaking message. She asked David to forgive her husband's reckless insults. ("He's like that with everybody," she said.) David did not need to engage in pointless bloodshed, she argued, for God would take care of the situation. David listened to Abigail's advice and decided not to harm Nabal.

4. Burdened, But Still Bold

Though David was still on the run, he had lost none of his courage. 1 Samuel 26 records yet another time when David boldly approached King Saul. Saul set up camp with three thousand soldiers. When night came, Saul was sleeping inside the camp surrounded by his armed guards, with his own spear stuck in the ground near his head.

David and a friend named Abishai decided to sneak into the campground. Silently, they crept unnoticed past the sleeping soldiers until they saw where Saul was sleeping on the ground. In an excited whisper, Abishai offered to kill Saul while he had the perfect opportunity. But David wouldn't allow it. He told Abishai, "Don't destroy him! Who can lay a hand on the Lord's anointed and be guiltless?" (1 Samuel 26:5–9).

TAKING THE NEXT STEP

Psalm and Sharing
8–12 Minutes

Even when life seems to be caving in around us, God remains the same and is worthy of our trust. Have someone read Psalm 57. Based on this psalm, written while David was fleeing from Saul, have class members share practical ways we can withstand the pressures and trials of life. Close in a time of prayer, praising God for being our deliverer from any trial we may face.

Groups

BUILDING COMMUNITY

1. Have group members respond to the following discussion starter: **Remember a time when you moved. What was it like? What was the most difficult aspect of your move?**

2. OPTION: Begin the group with the following word association: **What images come to mind when you hear the word** *cave*?

CONSIDERING SCRIPTURE

Read 1 Samuel 22:1–5.

1. Is God providing for David in these verses? If so, how?

2. During difficult times, it is easy to become self-absorbed. How did David respond to his circumstances?

3. When difficult times arise in your life, do you focus solely on yourself, or do you continue to care about others?

Read 1 Samuel 24:1–13.

4. How do you think David felt knowing three thousand chosen men were after him?

5. David had a chance to kill his enemy Saul in the cave but did not. Did David do the right thing? Why or why not?

6. Verse 8 records that David called out to Saul and bowed down in deference to him. Are you surprised that David continued to respect Saul despite the treatment Saul had given him?

7. How does David's interaction with Saul in this passage illustrate his faith and trust in God?

Accountability Partners

Have partners respond to the following questions: (1) Is there an unresolved conflict with another person in your life? (2) How have you handled that conflict so far? (3) What one thing can you do differently as you interact with this person based on the example of David's interaction with Saul?

OPTION
Worship Ideas

Read Psalm 57 together. Note the recurring refrain: "Be exalted, O God, above the heavens; let your glory be over all the earth" (Psalm 57:5, 11). Spend some time as a group praising God based on Psalm 57, for God truly is worthy of our praise among the nations.

OPTION
Memory Verse

"May the Lord judge between you and me. And may the Lord avenge the wrongs you have done to me, but my hand will not touch you" (1 Samuel 24:12).

TAKING THE NEXT STEP

1. Describe one time in your life when you have been "in the cave." When have you found yourself in a pit of despair or discouragement?

2. What pressures in your life right now are holding you down or keeping you from fulfilling your full potential for God's service?

3. David repeatedly confronted Saul and defended his actions, but he never yielded to the temptation to seek revenge or be vindictive. How do you respond when others mistreat you? How can you be assertive without giving in to hatred or a desire for revenge?

Stor(m)y Time

*In the space provided, write a very short story
about the most memorable storm you ever experienced.*

Discussion Questions

Read your assigned chapter. Then answer each of the following questions based on the chapter your group was assigned.

1. List the significant people discussed in this passage. What about each person's character or circumstances makes this person a significant part of the passage?

2. In four sentences or less, summarize the main events of the chapter.

3. What main challenges does David face in this chapter?

4. How does David respond to these challenges?

5. How is God involved in this passage?

6. List one practical way you can you apply the message of this passage to your lives.

Finding Purpose in the Pits

1. Attacked, But Not Alone

2. Victimized, But Not Vengeful

3. Angry, But Able to Accept Advice

4. Burdened, But Still Bold

Seven

Why Worry When You Can Worship?

Why worry when you can worship? Jesus said not to worry about our food, drink, and clothes, or even about our very lives; but he didn't stop there. Jesus went on to show that worship is a positive alternative to worry: "Seek ye first the kingdom of God" (Matthew 6:33, *King James Version*). The apostle Paul wrote, "Do not be anxious about anything." Then he continued, "But in everything, by prayer and petition, with thanksgiving, present your requests to God" (Philippians 4:6).

Why worry when you can worship? God's character holds the answers to our anxieties. Why worry about the future? God is timeless, eternal, the giver of hope. Why worry about finances? God is omnipotent, all-powerful, the giver of every perfect gift. Why worry about difficult relationships? God is love; he is the peacemaker and healer of wounds. Why worry even about death? We worship the immortal one, "the living God," the Almighty who has conquered sin and death through the resurrection of his Son.

—David Faust, *Praise Under Pressure*

Central Theme   God deserves our praise just because of who he is; but obedient, heartfelt worship also results in a positive by-product for the worshiper—greater freedom from worry.

Lesson Aim   Group members will identify specific ways to deepen their participation in worship and will recognize how God's praiseworthy qualities can help them overcome anxiety.

Bible Background   2 Samuel 6; Psalm 8

For Further Study   Read Chapter 7 in *Praise Under Pressure*.

 **lasses**

BUILDING COMMUNITY

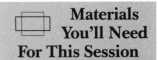 As class begins, divide participants into groups of five. Have them arrange their chairs into circles. Give each group a piece of poster board and a marker, and ask them to select one person as their "writer" or "secretary."

Ask the groups to write the words, *Why Worry?* at the top of one side of their poster, and the words, *Why Worship?* on the other side. Ask each group to list as many answers as possible for each question. Every person in the circle should offer at least one response to each of the questions. No one may offer a second answer until everyone in the circle has spoken at least once.

After about five minutes, ask the class, **Which of your lists is longer? Do we have more reasons to *worry* or to *worship*?** You may also want to ask, **Can you find any relationships between the two lists you've created?** (For example, the "Why Worry?" list may include "financial problems" or "fear of dying," while the "Why Worship?" list includes "God provides our needs" or "God is the source of life.")

As class begins, give each member a stick-on name tag and a pen. Ask each person to write his or her name on the name tag, plus a word or short phrase that describes his or her life during the past week. (For example: "Stressed," "Feeling Great!" "Tired," "On Vacation!" or "Worried") Leave space to write something else later in class (during the "Taking the Next Step" section). Participants should wear the name tags throughout the class.

Before class begins, write the following two sentences on the chalkboard: **"The more I worship, the less I worry"** and **"The more I worry, the less I worship."** Ask all of the class members to stand. Those who agree with the statements will move to one side of the room; those who disagree will go to the other side. Those who are undecided will stay in the middle of the room. Encourage at least two people in each group to explain their position.

Circle Response
8 Minutes

> **Materials You'll Need For This Session**
>
> Several pieces of poster board and markers (one poster and one marker for every five people in the class), chalkboard, chalk, stick-on name tags for each person in the class, pens, Resource Sheets 7A–7C, and Transparency 7A

OPTION
Name Tags
2–5 Minutes

OPTION
Agree-Disagree
8–10 Minutes

CONSIDERING SCRIPTURE

Introduction
2 Minutes

Lead into the Bible study by saying, **David's life teaches us a lot about how we can offer God true worship even when facing stress. Although David faced many pressures, we know him more for his worship than for his worries. Eventually, King Saul died in battle along with his sons, and David became king. One of David's first official acts as king had to do with worship. The ark of the covenant had been stored for safekeeping in the house of a man named Abinadab. David decided to bring the ark to his new capital city of Jerusalem (now known as the City of David). This was no small undertaking. David selected thirty thousand men to accompany the ark and assure its safe passage to Jerusalem. Second Samuel 6 tells what happened and reveals several important facts about meaningful worship. In our study today, we're going to see that worship is a healthy alternative to worry.**

OPTION
Focus Groups
15–20 Minutes

Distribute copies of <u>Resource Sheet 7A</u>. This worksheet is divided into four sections, each one dealing with a different aspect of 2 Samuel 6. Divide the class into four groups, and assign one section of the worksheet to each group. (Make sure each person has a pen or pencil, and a Bible.)

Ask two volunteers to read 2 Samuel 6 aloud to the entire class. (It's best to ask them ahead of time, so they can decide how to share the reading and handle unfamiliar words in the text.) As the Scripture is read, group members should watch for answers to the question they were assigned and write notes on their worksheets. After the Scripture is read, ask each group to spend five minutes discussing their notes and impressions among themselves. After five minutes, shuffle everyone into new groups composed of at least one person who answered question 1, one person who answered question 2, and so forth. Give the groups another five to seven minutes to share their notes and impressions.

OPTION
Lecture
15–20 Minutes

Distribute copies of <u>Resource Sheet 7B</u>, which lists three ways to make worship meaningful (taken from *Praise Under Pressure* by David Faust). Make sure all class members have a pen or pencil, and encourage them to write down any notes or questions that come to mind as you teach the Bible lesson from 2 Samuel 6. Ask volunteers to read the Scripture text before you comment on each section.

1. Hold God's Name in Awe (Volunteer reads 2 Samuel 6:1–5.) The ark of the covenant was a symbol of God's presence, protection, and mercy. It was "called by the Name, the name of the Lord Almighty, who is enthroned between the cherubim

that are on the ark" (2 Samuel 6:2). When the Israelites carried the ark from place to place, in a sense they were carrying the name of God with them.

We carry God's name with us too. We don't carry his name in a gold-covered box, but in our hearts! "We have this treasure in jars of clay to show that this all-surpassing power is from God and not from us" (2 Corinthians 4:7).

Imagine if all Christians wore name tags that said in bold letters, "Believe in Jesus," "Child of God," or "Follower of Christ." We don't wear name tags, but we are responsible to wear the Lord's name with dignity and reverence. . . . Do those around you catch a glimpse of the majesty of God's name?

2. Obey God's Word with Reverence (Volunteer reads 2 Samuel 6:6–11.)

At first glance God's abrupt death sentence seems unusually harsh. Why did God strike Uzzah down when he was only trying to help? David was angry, puzzled, and afraid. He suspended movement of the ark for three months while he pondered the situation (2 Samuel 6:8–11).

A closer examination of the circumstances makes it clear that God acted fairly—in fact, with remarkable patience. . . . In the Law of Moses, God gave specific instructions for the care of the ark (Numbers 3:27–31; 4:15–20). . . .

David's men flagrantly disregarded these guidelines. Placing the ark onto a new oxcart may have seemed like a nice gesture, but they weren't doing things the way God had prescribed. By using no poles, and by allowing ordinary men to touch the ark, they displayed too casual an attitude toward the holiness of God. Eventually, David realized the root of the problem, and he made sure that the ark was moved in accordance with God's instructions (1 Chronicles 15:1–15).

3. Celebrate God's Presence With Joy (Volunteer reads 2 Samuel 6:12–23.)

When David and his men followed God's instructions for carrying the ark, they found the freedom to worship with exuberance and joy. . . . Sacrifices were offered, and all the men and women present that day went home with a loaf of bread, a cake of dates, and a cake of raisins to eat. This worship celebration was anything but boring! God's people were filled with joy and excitement as they praised him from their hearts. . . .

[David's wife] Michal didn't seem to understand why the return of the ark was so significant, or why David loved God so much. She reminds us of Martha, who Jesus said was "worried and upset about many things," but whose worries made her overlook the one thing most needed—to worship at the feet of her Lord (Luke 10:38–42). David responded firmly to Michal's criticism. He insisted, "I will celebrate before the Lord" (2 Samuel 6:21). He was not worried about his own sense of dignity. Most of all, he just wanted to worship God.

TAKING THE NEXT STEP

Why Worship?
5–10 Minutes

Transparency 7A lists several reasons God deserves our worship, based on Psalm 8. Emphasize how it's better to focus on God's praiseworthy qualities than to be preoccupied with worry. Have class members look up and read aloud the Scripture texts listed on the transparency.

OPTION
Worship Self-Evaluation
5–10 Minutes

Resource Sheet 7C will lead class members to analyze their personal attitudes about worship. Distribute copies of the sheet, one per person. Make sure each participant has a pen or pencil. Allow them a minute or two to fill in the sheet, and then encourage several people to share what they wrote and why.

OPTION
Name Tag Additions
5–10 Minutes

If class members are wearing name tags (as suggested at the beginning of this lesson), ask each person to write an additional word or phrase on the name tag which describes or illustrates his or her relationship with God (for example, "Believer in Jesus," "Seeker for Truth," "Child of God," "Unsure," "Eager to Know More," "Christ Follower"). Encourage some of the participants to explain what they wrote. In the closing prayer, ask God to help us worship him more and worry less.

Groups

BUILDING COMMUNITY

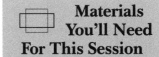

Materials You'll Need For This Session

Bibles, note cards, pens or pencils, Resource Sheet 7C

1. Give each person a note card and a pen or pencil. On one side of the card, group members should write the question, "Why Worry?" On the other side, write, "Why Worship?" **List as many answers as you can for each question.** Discuss: **Which list is longer? Is it easier to worry or to worship?**

2. OPTION Ask participants either to agree or disagree with the following statement: **The more I worship, the less I worry. The more I worry, the less I worship.**

3. OPTION **Describe the most memorable time of worship you have ever experienced. Where were you? What made this time of worship especially meaningful?**

CONSIDERING SCRIPTURE

Read 2 Samuel 6:1–5.

1. Why was moving the ark of God such a major event? Why were 30,000 men needed to move it?

Read 2 Samuel 6:6–11.

2. Why did Uzzah die? (Compare Numbers 3:27–31; 4:15–20; and 1 Chronicles 15:1–15.)

3. How do you feel about the death of Uzzah?

 a. **Uzzah deserved it.**
 b. **The punishment doesn't seem to fit the crime.**
 c. **God's action seems unusually harsh.**
 d. **I don't understand it, but I trust God's judgment.**
 e. **Other: _____.**

4. How did David respond to the death of Uzzah?

Read 2 Samuel 6:12–15, 17–19.

OPTION
Accountability Partners
Share with one an-
other your answers to
these questions:
(1) What is the biggest
worry you have
encountered during
the last week? (2) Is
there a way your partner
can help you deal with
this problem?

OPTION
Worship Ideas
Base your worship on
the theme, "How
majestic is your name
in all the earth!" List
several names or titles of
God (Savior, Father,
Redeemer, The Most
High). Offer specific
prayers of praise,
honoring God for who
God is and what God
has done.

OPTION
Memory Verse
"O Lord, our Lord, how
majestic is your name
in all the earth!"
(Psalm 8:1).

5. How would you describe David's worship before God? What actions and emotions demonstrated his love for God?

6. How does your own worship compare to David's?

Read 2 Samuel 6:16, 20–23.

7. Why was Michal so upset with David?

8. Are you satisfied with the way David responded to her criticism?

Read Psalm 8.

9. It's clear that David possessed a deep appreciation for God. What praiseworthy qualities of God do you see in this psalm?

10. Do you agree with the concept that worship is a helpful remedy for worry? How might this work in real life?

TAKING THE NEXT STEP

1. Give every member of the group a copy of <u>Resource Sheet 7C</u>. **Ask participants to fill in the Worship Self-Evaluation, and then share and explain their answers to the group.**

2. How does it help you personally to know that God is "mindful" of you (Psalm 8:4)?

3. What is the next step you need to take to grow in your personal worship of God?

4. In chapter seven of *Praise Under Pressure*, **the author suggests that "God's character holds the answers to our anxieties." Which of God's character qualities could be most helpful in dealing with your specific need? (For example, if you struggle with loneliness, you could praise God for always being present; if you are worried about a difficult decision, you could praise God as the source of wisdom.)**

Focus Groups

2 Samuel 6:1–23

1. What does this chapter tell us about <u>God</u>?

2. What <u>emotions</u> did David experience?

3. What are some ways David <u>worshiped</u> God?

4. What <u>problems</u> did David overcome?

Make Worship Meaningful

2 Samuel 6:1–23

- **Hold God's Name in Awe (verses 1–5)**

- **Obey God's Word with Reverence (verses 6–11)**

- **Celebrate God's Presence with Joy (verses 12–23)**

Worship Self-Evaluation

Honestly, which person in 2 Samuel 6 is <u>most like me</u>?

_____ I am like Uzzah. Lately I've been a little too casual about obeying God's Word. This chapter is a wake-up call, reminding me to be obedient even in "small things."

_____ I am like Michal. Lately I've been taking the critic's role. Instead of worshiping God with my whole heart, I have been focusing on other people and the things that bother me about them.

_____ I am like Obed-Edom the Gittite (see 2 Samuel 6:10–12). In a sense, my life is quiet, unspectacular, and ordinary. Yet the Lord has blessed me abundantly.

_____ I am like David. I am determined to worship God with my whole heart—not distracted by my own worries, and not discouraged by what others say or do.

God Deserves Our Worship!

GOD'S CHARACTER

"O Lord, our Lord, how majestic is your name in all the earth!" (Psalm 8:1).

- Exodus 34:4–7
- Psalm 145:8–14
- James 1:16, 17

GOD'S CREATIVITY

"When I consider your heavens, the work of your fingers, the moon and the stars, which you have set in place . . ." (Psalm 8:3).

- Psalm 104:10–26
- Colossians 1:15–17
- Hebrews 11:1–3

GOD'S CONCERN

"What is man that you are mindful of him, the son of man that you care for him?" (Psalm 8:4).

- Psalm 103:1–12
- Matthew 6:25–34
- 1 Peter 5:6, 7

Eight

Fit for a King: Honoring God in Times of Success

*E*ventually many of us achieve some measure of success. After years of expensive study, you finally graduate from college. Or you meet the right person and marry. You buy a house or receive a long-awaited promotion or enjoy that dream vacation you've always talked about. What then? What will happen when you finally attain the success you've been pursuing for so long?

David encountered many problems and stresses. But 2 Samuel 7 describes a time in David's life when everything was going well.

—David Faust, *Praise Under Pressure*

Central Theme	When life is filled with success, God must not be forgotten, for good times are a gift of God.
Lesson Aim	Participants will examine how David handled success and will learn how to handle success in a godly fashion.
Bible Background	2 Samuel 7, 8; Psalm 16
For Further Study	Read Chapter 8 in *Praise Under Pressure*.

 **Classes**

| Materials You'll Need For This Session |

Chalk and chalkboard,
Resource Sheets 8A–8C,
Transparency 8A

BUILDING COMMUNITY

Pass out copies of <u>Resource Sheet 8A</u>, the "Personal Success Inventory." Have participants complete the inventory on their own. After about five minutes, have some class members share which accomplishment would make them feel most successful and which accomplishment would mean very little to them. After a few minutes of sharing, say, **We all want success, and from time to time many of us enjoy some degree of success in life. While David endured many difficult times, he also was no stranger to success.**

Personal Success Inventory
10 Minutes

Before participants arrive, write at the top of the chalkboard, "Successful People." When students arrive, as a class compile a list of names of living people they consider successful. Write the names mentioned on the chalkboard. After several names are on the board, ask participants, **What do these people have in common?** After several responses, ask the class, **In what ways are some of these successful people different from some of the others?** Lead into "Considering Scripture" by saying, **Success can be defined in many different ways, but success in the world's eyes is not necessarily success in God's eyes. Yet in David we see a person who handled worldly success in such a way that, even in the midst of his success, his life was pleasing to God.**

OPTION
Successful People
10 Minutes

CONSIDERING SCRIPTURE

Pass out copies of <u>Resource Sheet 8B</u>, "Communication With God." Have the class divide into groups of four to work through this worksheet. After about twenty minutes, call the groups back together and have each group share its findings.

Small Group Study
30 Minutes

Divide the class into two groups. Have group A read 2 Samuel 7 and have group B read 2 Samuel 8. After each group has read its passage, have participants write down the different examples of success David experienced in their passage. After ten minutes, call the groups together and have each group share its findings. Then say to the class, **The real test for David was not that he had success, but how he handled it.** Display

OPTION
Team Work and Mini-Lecture
30 Minutes

Transparency 8A, "How David Handled Success." Use the following quotes from David Faust in *Praise Under Pressure* to elaborate on each point.

1. He Prayed About It.
As soon as he heard Nathan's encouraging words, "King David went in and sat before the Lord" (2 Samuel 7:18). His first response to success was not to gloat, pat himself on the back, or brag to a friend. He didn't even take his family out to dinner to celebrate! His first response was to pray.

2. He Was Humble About It.
David prayed, "Who am I, O Sovereign Lord, and what is my family, that you have brought me this far?" (2 Samuel 7:18). He realized, "apart from [the Lord] I have no good thing" (Psalm 16:2). David's success didn't swell his head with pride. He wasn't arrogant and boastful. He felt deeply unworthy of God's blessing.

3. He Viewed His Success as an Opportunity to Honor God.
David's prayer continued: "And now, Lord God, keep forever the promise you have made concerning your servant and his house. Do as you promised, so that your name will be great forever. Then men will say, 'The Lord Almighty is God over Israel!'" (2 Samuel 7:25, 26). David's goal was not just to make a name for himself. He wanted the Lord's name to be glorified.

TAKING THE NEXT STEP

How Do You Spell Success ?
10 Minutes

Have the class break into groups of four. Pass out Resource Sheet 8C. Have each group discuss what success means to them in a variety of important areas of their lives. Also, have groups wrestle with the question, **How is my view of success similar to and different from God's view of success?**

Groups

BUILDING COMMUNITY

1. Have group members respond to the question, **What is your number one goal in life?**

2. OPTION: Have group members share their responses to the following series of questions: **Describe one time when you accomplished a goal you had set for yourself. How did you feel? What did you do to celebrate?**

CONSIDERING SCRIPTURE

Read 2 Samuel 7:1–17.

1. Why do you think David was troubled by the fact that he had a palace while the ark of God remained in a tent?

2. Does God need or desire a house to dwell in? Why or why not?

3. What blessings did God promise David in this passage?

Read 2 Samuel 7:18–29.

4. How did David respond to God's word brought to him by the prophet Nathan?

5. In these verses, David was praying to God. What can we learn about prayer from David's example?

Accountability Partners

Discuss with your partner the main goals that you have for your life. Have you attained any of these goals? If so, how are you handling this success? If not, how are you preparing to handle success in a godly fashion?

OPTION
Worship Ideas

David's prayer in 2 Samuel 7:18–29 is one of thanksgiving and praise. As Christians, we often fail to give God thanks for the many blessings God bestows upon us. Go around the group and give each person a chance to share at least one thing he or she is thankful for. After everyone has shared, sing the praise chorus, "Give Thanks." Conclude with a prayer of thanksgiving.

OPTION
Memory Verse

"David reigned over all Israel, doing what was just and right for all his people" (2 Samuel 8:15).

Read 2 Samuel 8:13–15.

6. How would you describe David's life based on these verses? Explain.
   a. Charmed
   b. It doesn't get any better than this
   c. Born at the right time
   d. The world is his oyster
   e. Other: _____

7. In the midst of tremendous success and "victory wherever he went," how does David treat his people?

TAKING THE NEXT STEP

1. Is it possible for a Christian to be ambitious and goal-oriented without being selfish and egotistical? Explain.

2. In this passage, God and David communicate with one another. Do you communicate with God regularly? If not, what steps can you take to make prayer and communicating with God a priority in your life? If you do pray regularly, what is it like? What can you do to make your prayer life more like David's?

3. Even in a time of success, David did "what was just and right for all his people" (2 Samuel 8:15). Could the same be said of your relationships with others? What steps can you take this week to be just and to do right in all your relationships?

Personal Success Inventory

What would make you feel successful? Below is a list of ten achievements that would make some people feel successful. Rank the following accomplishments from 1 to 10 according to how important they are to whether you feel successful or not, with 1 being most important and 10 being least important.

___ a. Graduating summa cum laude from Princeton University

___ b. Receiving an annual salary of more than $100,000

___ c. Owning a Jeep Grand Cherokee to drive around town

___ d. Playing professional baseball for the Cleveland Indians

___ e. Owning a four-bedroom house with a two-car garage

___ f. Being invited to the White House to visit with the President of the United States

___ g. Having children who become successful in their own right

___ h. Writing a book about your favorite topic

___ i. Being recognized with a feature article in the local newspaper

___ j. Being named *Time* magazine's "Person of the Year"

Communication With God

Have a volunteer in your group read 2 Samuel 7. This passage is basically a conversation between God and David: God speaks to David through the prophet Nathan, and David speaks to God through prayer. Spend the next several minutes looking at the content of this conversation. Write a short paragraph summarizing what God is saying to David and how David responds to God.

GOD'S WORD TO DAVID

DAVID'S PRAYER TO GOD

How Do You Spell Success?

Success is defined differently by different people. What would make you feel successful? In each of the following categories, write what it would take to be a success in your own eyes. After you have responded to each category, share your answers with your group. How do your responses compare with God's ideas of success?

Career:

Friendships:

Family:

Child of God:

How David Handled
Success

1. **He Prayed About It.**

2. **He Was Humble About It.**

3. **He Viewed His Success as an Opportunity to Honor God.**

Nine

Dining at the King's Table

Much of the pressure we face in life comes from the outside—for example, as we deal with angry people or problems outside our control. Many times, however, the pressure comes from inside ourselves. A lot of stress is self-inflicted.

To a certain extent, it's good to recognize our weaknesses and imperfections. "Blessed are the poor in spirit, for theirs is the kingdom of heaven" (Matthew 5:3). Happy are those who sometimes feel unhappy with themselves, for only a humble, repentant heart can discover Heaven's kind of happiness!

We really aren't worthy—but we're not worthless. We can never do enough, work enough, or be good enough to earn God's favor—but God shows us kindness anyway. . . . God turns paupers into princes. He takes us from the gutter of sin and seats us at the King's table.

—David Faust, *Praise Under Pressure*

Central Theme	The grace of God can help us overcome our feelings of inadequacy and worthlessness.
Lesson Aim	By examining King David's kindness to Mephibosheth, participants will gain a deeper appreciation of God's grace and will identify ways to show kindness to others.
Bible Background	2 Samuel 9; Psalm 23
For Further Study	Read Chapter 9 in *Praise Under Pressure*.

Classes

BUILDING COMMUNITY

Before class, place a small wastebasket or trash can on a table in the classroom. Put a "treasure chest" (a foil-covered box) next to the trash can. Scatter on the table at least ten assorted household items. Suggestions: a small decorative candle, a small garden tool, a coffee mug, a refrigerator magnet, a framed photo of a family member, a T-shirt, a fancy dish or serving tray, an ice cream dipper, a baseball card, a TV remote control, a tape cassette or CD featuring a musical performer, a piece of jewelry.

Begin the class by holding up the household items one at a time. Ask the group to decide (by raising hands for a majority vote) whether each object is "trash" or "treasure." Place "trash" items into the trash can and "treasure" items into the treasure chest.

After all of the household items have been placed in the appropriate container, give each participant a note card and ask each person to write his or her name on the card. Tell the class: **During the past week, have you thought of yourself more as** *trash* **or as** *treasure*? Ask volunteers to step forward and place their name card in either the trash can or the treasure chest, and explain why they feel this way.

Give each member of the class a blank piece of paper, a crayon, and several dollars of pretend money (Monopoly money works fine). Allow everyone exactly one minute (time them!) to draw a picture. When a minute is over, announce that you're having an art auction. Select a volunteer (someone with a good sense of humor) to serve as an "auctioneer." See whose drawing brings the highest price. Ask the class, **How did it feel when others "devalued" your work of art by choosing some-one else's creation over yours? If you're not a very skilled artist, did you feel you had a fair chance in this competition?** Explain, **Sometimes it's hard to see the worth of another per-son's ideas or creations. Sometimes it's even difficult to see our own worth as a creation of God.**

Trash or Treasure?
10 Minutes

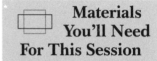

Materials You'll Need For This Session

Small wastebasket or trash can, "treasure chest" (a cardboard box covered with aluminum foil will work well), ten or more assorted household items for the "Trash or Treasure?" activity, note cards, pens or pencils, pretend "dollar bills" (or Monopoly money), crayons, Resource Sheets 9A and 9B, and Transparency 9A

OPTION
Art Auction
10 Minutes

CONSIDERING SCRIPTURE

During this part of the session you will lead the class in a study of *2 Samuel 9*, which tells the story of David's kindness to Mephibosheth. Display Transparency 9A, and comment briefly on each point. Here is a summary of what you might say, based on David Faust's comments in *Praise Under Pressure*:

It's not unusual to experience times when we feel like "trash" rather than "treasure." Some of us may struggle with self-esteem issues. Others may feel overworked and under-appreciated. Some of us may feel unhappy with something about our physical appearance, our personality, our job, or our status in life. Some of life's toughest pressures are self-inflicted. Our own sense of weakness and inadequacy can weigh us down and prevent us from serving the Lord effectively. Instead of feeling on top of the world, there are times when we feel the world is on top of us!

While we must not be prideful and overconfident about our abilities, we also must avoid going to the other extreme and concluding we are worthless. No human being is trash in the eyes of God! Second Samuel 9 tells the interesting story of King David's kindness to a man named Mephibosheth. This story provides a helpful illustration of the way God, our gracious king, treats us.

Mephibosheth Was . . . a Weak Man

• Son of David's friend Jonathan, who had been killed in battle (1 Samuel 31:2–6)
• Grandson of the disappointing former king, Saul
• Forced to live with physical complications ("crippled in both feet"; 2 Samuel 4:4; 9:3)
• Faced with social limitations (afraid of reprisals from King David, he lived in the obscure village of Lo Debar; 2 Samuel 9:4, 5)
• Saddled with limited expectations (saw himself as nothing but "a dead dog"; 2 Samuel 9:8)

David Was . . . a Kind King

• He wanted to show kindness (2 Samuel 9:1).
• He kept his promises (especially the commitment he had made to show kindness to the household of his friend Jonathan; 1 Samuel 20:42; 2 Samuel 9:1).
• He searched for someone to bless (2 Samuel 9:3–5).
• He treated Mephibosheth like part of his own family (even insisting he dine at David's family table; 2 Samuel 9:9–13).

Conclude by saying, **When you think about it, we all have something in common with Mephibosheth. He was weak; so are we. He was unworthy of the king's royal favors; so are we. Romans 5:10 indicates that our sin makes us enemies of God, yet through Jesus Christ he has treated us with amazing kindness and grace. We are unworthy servants, but Christ our King seeks the lost, adopts us into his family, and treats us like one of his own.**

Ask a volunteer who is an excellent reader to read aloud the story of David and Mephibosheth from *2 Samuel 9:1–13*. (Note: it's best to ask the volunteer a few days ahead, so she or he can become familiar with the story itself and the unfamiliar words found in this Scripture text.)

After the chapter is read, divide the class into two groups. Each group should select a discussion leader and a note taker to write down responses. Group One will focus on Mephibosheth: *Who was he? What problems did he face? Why did he feel like a "dead dog"? How do you think he felt about King David?* Group Two will focus on David: *Why did he search for Mephibosheth? What motivated him to show kindness to the grandson of his former enemy, Saul? Why did he decide to have Mephibosheth eat in his home? What was the significance of the king's table?*

After about ten minutes, ask each group to report their findings to the entire class. You may want to display Transparency 9A and use it to reinforce some of the groups' comments.

OPTION
Buzz Groups
20–25 Minutes

TAKING THE NEXT STEP

Give all participants a copy of Resource Sheet 9A. Ask them to read through section A and place a check mark next to the statement that identifies an area of personal weakness in their lives. After one to two minutes, the class will divide into groups of three and discuss the questions in section B of the worksheet.

Weakness Inventory
10 Minutes

Distribute copies of Resource Sheet 9B. Brainstorm with the group about individuals or groups of people in your community who need to experience kindness from God's people. **Who, like Mephibosheth, needs to be sought out, encouraged, welcomed, and fed? What specific steps can you take to meet these needs?**

Conclude the class by Reading Psalm 23 and leading in prayer.

OPTION
**To Whom Can
I Show Kindness?**
10 Minutes

Groups

BUILDING COMMUNITY

1. **What memories—good, bad, or humorous—do you have of your family dinner table when you were growing up?**

2. OPTION: **Do you enjoy garage sales? Why or why not? Why is it that "one person's trash is another person's treasure"?**

3. OPTION: **What is your most valuable possession? What is your *least* valuable possession?**

CONSIDERING SCRIPTURE

Read 2 Samuel 9:1–13.

1. **Why was David so interested in showing kindness to someone descended from King Saul? Wasn't Saul his former enemy?** (Compare 1 Samuel 20:42.)

2. **Why was Mephibosheth crippled in both feet? What caused this problem?** (See 2 Samuel 4:4.)

3. **What was it like to face a physical challenge like this one in biblical times? How did people in similar circumstances cope with their problems?** (Compare Mark 2:3; Acts 3:2.)

4. **How do *you* treat people who struggle with physical or emotional weaknesses?**

5. **How do you think Mephibosheth felt when he first learned that David was summoning him to the palace? Why was he so afraid?**

6. **Why did Mephibosheth refer to himself as "a dead dog" (verse 8)?**
    a. **He suffered from very low self-esteem.**
    b. **He was merely showing respect and deference to the king.**
    c. **He considered himself unclean, and a dog was a Hebrew symbol for uncleanness.**
    d. **Other:** _____

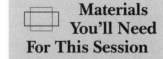

Materials You'll Need For This Session

Bibles, Resource Sheets 9A and 9B, pens or pencils

Accountability Partners

Partners should complete one of these sentences: **"Sometimes I feel inadequate because . . ."** or **"My greatest area of weakness right now is . . ."** Ask God to sustain your partner through God's grace and strength.

OPTION
Worship Ideas

Read Psalm 23 out loud, but personalize the psalm by inserting names of group members wherever the word "I," "my," or "me" appears. For example, "The Lord is John's shepherd, Mary shall lack nothing. He makes Bill lie down in green pastures, he leads Susan beside quiet waters . . ."

OPTION
Memory Verse

"You prepare a table before me in the presence of my enemies. You anoint my head with oil, my cup overflows" (Psalm 23:5).

7. Why did David invite Mephibosheth to eat in his home? Why not provide for him in some other way?

8. Was there some special significance to eating at the king's table? (Compare 1 Kings 2:7; 18:19.)

9. Do you see any parallels between the way David treated Mephibosheth and the way God treats us?

10. Does Jesus, our King, invite us to dine at *his* family table? In what sense? (Compare Psalm 23:5; Luke 12:35–38; Revelation 3:20; 19:9.)

TAKING THE NEXT STEP

1. Give everyone a copy of <u>Resource Sheet 9A</u>. Ask participants to read through section A and place a check mark next to the statement that identifies an area of personal weakness in their lives. After one to two minutes, divide into groups of three or four and discuss the questions in section B of the worksheet.

2. OPTION: Distribute copies of <u>Resource Sheet 9B</u>. Ask, **Is it time for our small group to undertake a ministry project?** Brainstorm with the group about persons in your community who need to be sought out, encouraged, welcomed, or fed in Jesus' name.

Weakness Inventory

Many times we hesitate to think about our weaknesses, preferring instead to focus on our areas of strength. The apostle Paul offered a thought-provoking perspective, however, when he wrote, "For Christ's sake, I delight in weaknesses, in insults, in hardships, in persecutions, in difficulties. For when I am weak, then I am strong" (2 Corinthians 12:10).

SECTION A. Place a check mark next to one of the following areas of weakness that has made your life more difficult:

____ A *bodily* weakness (illness, injury, or other physical complication)

____ A *social* limitation (such as growing up in an unhappy family, difficulty with friendships, trouble finding acceptance from others)

____ A *financial* hardship (loss of job, long-standing indebtedness, an unexpected bill to pay)

____ An *educational* struggle (learning problem, poor school system, limited opportunities)

____ An *emotional* burden (depression, anger, grief, loneliness, fear)

____ Other: _____

SECTION B. Discuss in groups of three:

1. Has God helped you cope with this area of weakness? How?

2. How has (or could) a Christian sister or brother help you bear this burden?

To Whom Can I Show Kindness?

(2 Samuel 9:1)

David actively sought out a person in need. He didn't merely sit back and talk about showing kindness. He took active steps to find Mephibosheth and bring him into the palace.

WHO?

Are there individuals or groups in our community to whom we could show kindness for the Lord's sake? Who is being overlooked?

HOW?

What specific steps can we take to meet these needs?

WHEN?

When shall we undertake this ministry project?

A Weak Man ... A Kind King

MEPHIBOSHETH'S WEAKNESSES:

- Physical complications (2 Samuel 4:4; 9:3)

- Social limitations (2 Samuel 9:4, 5)

- Limited expectations (2 Samuel 9:8)

DAVID'S KIND DEEDS:

- He wanted to show kindness (2 Samuel 9:1).

- He kept his promises (1 Samuel 20:42; 2 Samuel 9:1).

- He searched for someone to bless (2 Samuel 9:3–5).

- He treated Mephibosheth like part of the family
  (2 Samuel 9:9–13).

Ten

The High Price of Giving In

One of the most famous statues in the world stands on display in Florence, Italy. It is a statue of King David. In the early 1500s, Michelangelo took two and one-half years to carve a great work of art out of a thirteen and a half foot high block of marble. Michelangelo saw David as the true Renaissance man, the ideal human being: strong, confident, rock-like, determined, heroic.

But 2 Samuel 11 and 12 reveals a disappointing side of David's life. Like the rest of us, this great man wasn't chiseled out of marble after all. In a weak moment, David yielded to sexual temptation and committed adultery, and then he engaged in a deadly cover-up scheme. It is a true-life story of a sin committed, a sin confronted, and a sin confessed.

—Adapted from David Faust, *Praise Under Pressure*

Central Theme	King David's moral failure not only demonstrates the tragic consequences of disobedience; it also provides a helpful model for confronting, confessing, and conquering sin through the grace and power of God.
Lesson Aim	Participants will be able to overcome temptation through increased spiritual discernment, personal accountability, and prayer.
Bible Background	2 Samuel 11, 12; Psalm 51
For Further Study	Read Chapter 10 in *Praise Under Pressure*.

PLAN ONE

Classes

BUILDING COMMUNITY

Before class, prepare an appealing but not-very-healthy dessert (for example, chocolate cake) and a healthy but less exciting snack (for example, broccoli or celery sticks). Make sure there is enough of each item for the entire class to share. Select two volunteers to engage in a silent debate. Explain that each person in the class may select and eat only *one* food item, either the healthy snack or the unhealthy dessert. The debaters may use gestures, but no words. *Without speaking*, one volunteer will try to persuade members of the class to select the rich dessert, while the other volunteer will try to persuade everyone to choose the healthy snack.

While everyone eats the food items selected, talk about these questions: **(1) Why do we sometimes make choices we know aren't good for us? (2) Why are some temptations easy to resist? Why are other temptations so difficult to resist?**

CONSIDERING SCRIPTURE

Lead into the Bible study by explaining, **God's Word is always honest. The Bible realistically describes human weaknesses and provides some vivid stories about people who yielded to temptation. Even great heroes of the faith sometimes made huge mistakes. For example, the Bible tells us bluntly about Noah's drunkenness, Moses' anger, and Peter's denials of Christ. Today we're going to study the Bible's disappointing but true-to-life account of King David's adulterous affair with a woman named Bathsheba. David's story can help us overcome temptation in our own lives.**

Divide the class into six small groups. Provide each group a copy of Resource Sheet 10A, which contains six study questions. Assign each group one of the questions to study and discuss. After eight to ten minutes, ask each group to report their findings to the entire class. Present Transparency 10A. Cover the transparency with a sheet of paper and reveal one point at a time as each group gives its report. Distribute copies of Resource Sheet 10B. Summarize the lesson by discussing how the story of David portrays both a violation of God's standards and a demonstration of God's grace.

Silent Debate
6–8 Minutes

> ### Materials You'll Need For This Session
>
> An appealing but unhealthy dessert (for example, chocolate cake), a healthy but less exciting food (for example, broccoli or celery sticks), Resource Sheets 10A–10C, Transparency 10A, pens or pencils

Small Groups
25–30 Minutes

Provide a brief (five to seven minute) overview of 2 Samuel 11 and 12, using <u>Transparency 10A</u>, "The Cycle of Sin," and ideas found in Chapter Ten of *Praise Under Pressure*. Divide the class into four groups. Ask each group to focus on one of the following four persons: David (2 Samuel 11:1–15; 12:15–25); Bathsheba (2 Samuel 11:1–15, 26, 27; 12:15–25); Uriah the Hittite (2 Samuel 11:1–15); and Nathan the prophet (2 Samuel 11:26, 27; 12:1–15).

Each group will select a volunteer to role play the character assigned and will help prepare the person for the role play by talking about the character's actions and motivations. What role did this person play in the story? Why did this person do what he or she did? After about ten minutes of discussion, the four volunteers each will present a two- to three-minute role play to the entire class. (The teacher of the class may wish to "interview" each of the characters.) Distribute copies of <u>Resource Sheet 10B</u>. Summarize the lesson by discussing how the story of David portrays both a violation of God's standards and a demonstration of God's grace.

TAKING THE NEXT STEP

Distribute copies of <u>Resource Sheet 10C</u>, "The Challenge of Sexual Purity." This worksheet asks participants to think about specific ways to deal with sexual temptations like the kind David experienced. Ask participants to write at least one sentence under each of the three categories. After two to three minutes, ask participants to share their answers with the person sitting next to them. (It may be best to group the class according to gender for this portion of the class: men with men, women with women.) After about five minutes, ask volunteers to share some of their responses with the entire class.

Conclude the class by asking two or three volunteers to read Psalm 51. Allow time for silent prayer, and encourage participants to silently confess their sins to God. Ask a volunteer to voice a prayer of corporate confession. Pray for strength to overcome temptation, and include thanksgiving for God's mercy and forgiveness.

Groups

BUILDING COMMUNITY

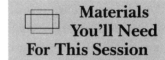
Materials You'll Need For This Session

Bibles, note cards, pens or pencils

1. In *Praise Under Pressure*, David Faust says, "Our world is littered with spiritual land mines. Some of Satan's weapons are easy to recognize, but others are like explosive land mines hidden just beneath the surface." Begin the meeting by asking each group member to write on a note card one temptation he or she considers a "spiritual land mine" in today's world. Collect and shuffle the cards, and then hand a card to each participant. Each person should read the card and tell how he or she would react if faced with that particular temptation.

2. OPTION: Ask each participant to describe a childhood incident when he or she disobeyed a parent or a teacher and was caught in the act.

CONSIDERING SCRIPTURE

Read 2 Samuel 11:1–5.

1. Why do you suppose David stayed in Jerusalem during the season when kings usually went off to war?

2. Why do you think David decided to sleep with Bathsheba? What was he thinking?
   a. I'm king and I'll do as I please.
   b. I'm bored and she's beautiful.
   c. What can I say? Spring is the season for romance!
   d. He didn't think at all; he just acted on impulse.

3. Why is it that even a dedicated follower of God like David was susceptible to sexual sin at this point in his life?

4. According to 1 Corinthians 10:13, God always provides a way of escape when we are tempted. How could David have handled his feelings toward Bathsheba without giving in to sin?

Read 2 Samuel 11:6–17.

5. What strategies did David employ to cover up his sin?

6. What strategies do you sometimes employ to cover up your sin?

7. What word would you use to describe David's character based on these verses? Uriah's character?

Read 2 Samuel 12:1–13.

8. How do you feel about Nathan's role in this incident?

9. What can we learn from the way Nathan confronted David's sin?

10. How do you feel about confronting others who are involved in immoral or destructive behavior?

11. How did David respond to his own sin once he was made aware of it? (See 2 Samuel 12:13; Psalm 51:1, 2.)

TAKING THE NEXT STEP

1. Describe one time in your life when you totally "blew it" and had to face your own failure. What happened? How did you handle it?

Read Psalm 51.

2. What is your favorite verse in this chapter? How does David's heartfelt confession speak to your own heart?

3. How does God's grace help us overcome even life's most embarrassing and painful experiences?

The High Price of Giving In

1. Read 2 Samuel 11:1–5. What was going on in David's life that made him susceptible to this temptation?

2. Read 2 Samuel 11:6–17. In addition to adultery, what sin(s) did David commit? How did his problems grow more complicated as he tried to cover up his initial mistake?

3. Read 2 Samuel 11:14–17, 26, 27; 12:9–18. What were the consequences of David's sins? What people were affected by his decisions?

4. Read 2 Samuel 12:1–14. What technique(s) did Nathan use in confronting David's sin? What can we learn from this courageous confrontation?

5. Read 2 Samuel 12:13 and Psalm 51:1–9. What was David's initial response when Nathan the prophet confronted him about his sin? What feelings do you think he was experiencing as he confessed his sin? Do you see any indications that his repentance was genuine and heartfelt—not merely a reaction to being "caught"?

6. Read Psalm 51:7–17. Could David really expect to be forgiven? How could his sins be cleansed? Could he still be a useful servant of God after what he had done?

Learning to Follow God's Standards and Trust in God's Grace

GOD'S STANDARDS VIOLATED

David sinned *by*:
- committing adultery (2 Samuel 11:2–5; compare Exodus 20:14, 17)
- attempting to cover up his offense (2 Samuel 11:6–13; Proverbs 28:13)
- arranging for the death of Uriah (2 Samuel 11:14–17; Proverbs 6:17)

David sinned *against*:
- Bathsheba
- Uriah
- the people of Israel (Proverbs 14:34; 16:12)
- the Lord (2 Samuel 11:27; Psalm 51:4)
- himself (Proverbs 6:32; 1 Corinthians 6:18)

GOD'S GRACE DEMONSTRATED

God showed grace by:
- sending the prophet Nathan to confront David (2 Samuel 12:1–12)
- showing love for David's son, Solomon (2 Samuel 12:24, 25; 1 Kings 1–11)
- forgiving David's sins (2 Samuel 12:13; Psalm 32:1–7; Psalm 51:1, 2, 7–12)

THE CHALLENGE OF
Sexual Purity

SET STANDARDS.

In this space, write one specific standard of behavior—a definite moral boundary—God has set in regard to sexual behavior.

ENCOURAGE PURITY.

In this space, write one specific way Christians can encourage one another in a positive way and hold one another accountable to a lifestyle of sexual purity.

EXPECT TO BE TESTED.

In this space, write one specific way Christians today may find their sexual purity tested.

The Cycle of Sin

(James 1:14, 15)

THE UPWARD SPIRAL

THE DOWNWARD SPIRAL

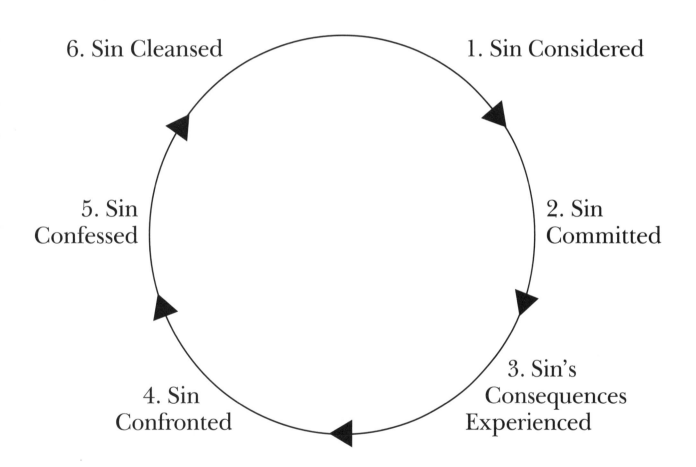

6. Sin Cleansed

1. Sin Considered

5. Sin Confessed

2. Sin Committed

4. Sin Confronted

3. Sin's Consequences Experienced

Eleven

Heartbreak in the Household

Many of us experience pain in our households. Some of our deepest wounds come from our nearest relatives. For many folks, the word "family" brings to mind a lot of pressure, frustration, and guilt.

God's Word is bluntly honest about this. Parental favoritism (Isaac and Rebekkah), sibling rivalry (Jacob and Esau), infertility (Hannah), sexual promiscuity (Eli's sons), marital cruelty (Nabal and Abigail), and widowhood (the widow at Zarephath) are among the family problems mentioned in Scripture. But King David's family provides one of the most vivid examples of heartbreak in the home.

—David Faust, *Praise Under Pressure*

Central Theme   God desires us to be actively involved in our families, communicating love by dealing appropriately with sin and conflict, by listening sensitively to the needs of other family members, and by being an agent of mercy, forgiveness, and compassion.

Lesson Aim   By examining David's role in his family, class members will be challenged to carefully consider ways they can be more godly family members.

Bible Background   2 Samuel 13–18; Psalm 3

For Further Study   Read Chapter 11 in *Praise Under Pressure*.

PLAN ONE

Classes

BUILDING COMMUNITY

Many political figures, religious leaders, and social scientists have talked of the decay of the family. Spend the first few moments of class brainstorming as a class on the question, **What are the top three reasons families are in so much trouble?**

Lead into Bible study by saying, **It is relatively easy to point out the flaws so prevalent in the American family. In many of our own families, we experience pain as well as joy. Yet family dysfunctions are not new in the late twentieth century. In fact, David himself had more than his share of family problems. Let us examine the Scripture together.**

Pass out copies of <u>Resource Sheet 11A</u>. Divide the class into groups of two. Have participants work through the worksheet and then share their pictures with their partners. Call the class back together and say, **All of us come from unique family situations. Some were very good and some were very difficult, but no family is perfect. In fact, David's family was far from perfect.**

CONSIDERING SCRIPTURE

Read *2 Samuel 13; 14:28–33; 18:32, 33* aloud. Then hand out copies of <u>Resource Sheet 11B</u>, "Fearsome Foursome." Have the class break into groups of four. Have them work through the questions together. After about twenty minutes, bring the class back together and spend a few minutes discussing their answers.

Ask for volunteers to read *2 Samuel 13; 14:28–33; and 18:32, 33*. Share with the class that **David's family certainly had its problems, but in many ways partial responsibility for these problems was David's lack of involvement and concern in the lives of his children.** Display <u>Transparency 11A</u>, which contains four points gleaned from *Praise Under Pressure* by David Faust. Discuss King David's role in his family struggles as you briefly highlight the following insights:

Brainstorming
8 Minutes

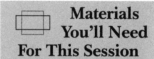

Materials You'll Need For This Session

Pens or pencils, chalkboard and chalk, Resource Sheets 11A–11C, Transparency 11A

OPTION
The Dinner Table
15 Minutes

Fearsome Foursomes
25–30 Minutes

OPTION
Mini-Lecture
25–30 Minutes

1. **David Failed to Confront Sin in His Family.**
When the Bible tells about Adonijah, another of David's sons, it says, "His father had never interfered with him by asking, 'Why do you behave as you do?'" (1 Kings 1:6). Doesn't it seem strange that this mighty leader of people failed to lead his own children well? Was he too tenderhearted to be firm with those he loved? Did he assume his job as a father was mainly just to provide material things for his children? Or was he simply too busy—distracted by all the demands of his job as king?

2. **David Failed to Communicate With His Family.**
David allowed an unhealthy distance to develop between himself and his children. He was easily deceived by Amnon's faked illness and naive when he failed to see Amnon's real motive in inviting Tamar to visit his bedroom. After Tamar was raped, David became angry but did not get involved.

3. **David Failed to Show Mercy and Forgiveness to Family Members.**
Absalom killed Amnon and went into hiding for three years in a place called Geshur. Though "the king longed to go to Absalom," there was no contact between them for a long time. Later Absalom moved back to Jerusalem, but "Absalom lived two years in Jerusalem without seeing the king's face" (2 Samuel 13:38, 39; 14:28). At least five years passed with little or no contact between David and Absalom. Meanwhile, old grievances grew, unhealed wounds festered, and angry feelings remained unresolved.

4. **The Result: Misery and Weeping.**
If David had clung to a shred of hope that Absalom would repent, now there was nothing left but grief. Despite all the harm Absalom had done, David still felt his son's loss with anguish only a parent can fully understand. With tears streaming down his cheeks, David grieved the loss of his wayward but beloved son: "O my son Absalom! My son, my son Absalom! If only I had died instead of you—O Absalom, my son, my son!" (2 Samuel 18:33).

TAKING THE NEXT STEP

David made many mistakes as a parent and husband, and he suffered the consequences; yet as he repented of these mistakes, God forgave and restored David. Spend some time as a class brainstorming creative ways to intentionally involve God in our families.

Involving God in Our Families
5–10 Minutes

Have each individual work through <u>Resource Sheet 11C</u>. After each person completes the sheet, have participants pair up and read their prayers to God.

PLAN TWO

roups

BUILDING COMMUNITY

1. Have participants share their responses to the following questions: **Describe a vacation or trip your family took when you were a child. Where did you go? What or who did you see? Did you have a good time?**

2. OPTION: **Many political figures, religious leaders, and social scientists have talked about the decay of the family in society. Why do you think families are in so much trouble?**

CONSIDERING SCRIPTURE

Read 2 Samuel 13:1–22.

1. What prompted Amnon to rape Tamar?

   a. Frustration
   b. Bad advice
   c. Lust
   d. A perverted need for power
   e. Other: _____

2. How did David respond to the news that Amnon had raped Tamar? Did he respond appropriately? Why or why not?

Read 2 Samuel 13:23–38.

3. How did Absalom respond to the rape of his sister, Tamar?

4. Was Absalom justified in killing Amnon? Why or why not?

Read 2 Samuel 14:28–33.

5. David did not see Absalom's face for more than five years after Absalom killed Amnon. How could David have dealt with his grief and anger in a healthier way within his family?

6. In 2 Samuel 15, we learn that Absalom successfully conspired to take the throne of Israel away from David. Given

Materials You'll Need For This Session

Resource Sheet 11C, pens or pencils

Accountability Partners

Have partners share their responses to this question: **We have seen the type of family member David was. What type of family member are you?** After each person has shared, have partners spend some time discussing ways they can be more Christlike in their families.

OPTION
Worship Ideas

One of the real joys of being a Christian is the fact that we are a part of the family of God. 1 John 3:1 states, "How great is the love the Father has lavished on us, that we should be called children of God! And that is what we are!" Spend some time in prayer, thanking God for our adoption as his sons and daughters through the death and resurrection of Jesus Christ.

OPTION
Memory Verse

"The king was shaken. He went up to the room over the gateway and wept. As he went, he said: 'O my son Absalom! My son, my son Absalom! If only I had died instead of you—O Absalom, my son, my son!'" (2 Samuel 18:33).

David's past relationship with his son Absalom, are you surprised by this? Why or why not?

Read 2 Samuel 18:19–33.

7. Eventually, Absalom and his followers are defeated by David's forces. David's expected excitement over his victory is overshadowed by his grief for Absalom. What does verse 33 reveal about David's relationship with his children?

8. Which phrase best describes the type of father David was?
   a. He had trouble expressing his feelings.
   b. Work came before family.
   c. He had regrets.
   d. He had no significant relationships with his kids.
   e. He was a reactive parent instead of a leader.
   f. He gave a little too little, a little too late.
   g. Other: _____

TAKING THE NEXT STEP

1. Which child of David's do you most relate with?
   a. Amnon: I have openly rebelled against God.
   b. Absalom: I often take matters into my own hands.
   c. Tamar: I'm paying the price for the mistakes of others.

2. What heartaches do you face in your family? What steps are you taking to deal with them?

3. Pass out copies of Resource Sheet 11C, "A Prayer for My Family," and have members complete it. After about ten minutes, give group members the option of reading their prayers during corporate prayer time.

The Dinner Table

The rectangle below represents a dinner table. On the dinner table, draw a place mat for each member of your family when you were a child. (Include parents, step-parents, siblings, and any others who lived in your house.) Write the name of the family member inside the place mat. Then draw lines between family members to denote the relationships they had with one another. For example, you might draw a solid, straight line between two family members who had a strong, positive relationship, while drawing a jagged line between two family members who had a difficult relationship. Be creative in the drawing of lines and as accurate as possible about the interpersonal relationships within your childhood home.

Fearsome Foursome

1. Why do you think Amnon raped Tamar?

2. How did David respond to the news that Amnon raped Tamar? How should he have responded?

3. Was Absalom justified in killing Amnon? Why or why not?

4. David did not see his son Absalom for more that five years after Absalom killed Amnon. How could David have dealt with his grief and anger in a healthier way within his family?

5. What does 2 Samuel 18:33 reveal about David's relationship with his children?

6. What phrase would you use to describe David as a father?
   a. He had trouble expressing his feelings.
   b. Work came before family.
   c. A little too little, a little too late.
   d. He had many regrets.
   e. He reacted to family crises instead of leading his family.
   f. Other: _____

A Prayer for My Family

No family is perfect. David is not alone when it comes to family dysfunction. Many have lingering pain from childhood family relationships that need attention. Many also have present areas of need regarding family relationships. David spent five years avoiding a family crisis. Don't make the same mistake. Instead, take your situation to God in prayer. Spend the next several minutes writing a prayer to God concerning your family situation in the space provided. It could be a prayer of thanksgiving, confession, healing, anger, intercession for a family member, or simply for the ability to hand a situation over to God.

Family PROBLEMS

1. David Failed to Confront Sin
in His Family.

2. David Failed to Communicate
With His Family.

3. David Failed to Show
Mercy and Forgiveness
to Family Members.

4. The Result:
Misery and Weeping.

Twelve

Mighty Men

King David faced a lot of pressure. But David offered God praise because the Lord had planted "glads" in his life. One of David's biggest reasons for gladness was a group of supportive friends who assisted him, fought for him, and sacrificed themselves for his benefit. Some of these fellows, known as David's mighty men, probably rose from the ranks of the four hundred "in distress or in debt or discontented" who originally gathered around David while he was being pursued by Saul (1 Samuel 22:2). Under David's leadership they became strong leaders themselves, and some of them became notable heroes. Second Samuel 23 records the exploits of David's mighty men.

—David Faust, *Praise Under Pressure*

Central Theme	David's mighty men were willing to serve others and God under any and all circumstances. One of the best ways for us to offer "praise under pressure" is by serving others through God's strength at all times.
Lesson Aim	Participants will examine their own willingness to serve God and others in their daily lives.
Bible Background	2 Samuel 23 and 24; Psalm 22
For Further Study	Read Chapter 12 *Praise Under Pressure*.

Classes

BUILDING COMMUNITY

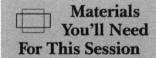 Before the class arrives, remove several chairs from the room so there will be far too few chairs to go around. Make sure that class members will not have easy access to chairs in nearby areas. When participants arrive, let them deal with this crisis on their own. Intentionally start the class a few minutes later than normal, giving the class time to respond to the lack of adequate seating. Once people have settled down, ask the class the following questions: **How did you feel when you saw there were not going to be enough chairs for everyone? Were any of you willing to sit on the floor so someone else could have a seat? Did anyone in the class become the "hero" by retrieving chairs for other class members from other parts of the building? In a situation like this, are you willing to sacrifice your comfort for the comfort of someone else?**

Lead into Scripture study by saying, **It is fairly easy to help others when it does not cost us anything. It is quite another matter when helping another person involves real sacrifice on our part. David's mighty men understood what real sacrifice is all about.**

On a chalkboard, write the word SACRIFICE across the top. When the class arrives, have them think of one- or two-word definitions for the word *sacrifice*. Write the responses on the board. After several minutes, lead into Scripture study by saying, **Whatever else you want to say about sacrifice, you have to admit that it isn't easy. Sacrifice is hard work and costly. Seldom are people truly sacrificial in their dealings with others, but David's mighty men certainly were. They risked their very lives for David's sake and for God's sake. Through their example, we can learn better how to be truly sacrificial in our service to God and others.**

CONSIDERING SCRIPTURE

Divide the class into six groups. Pass out copies of <u>Resource Sheet 12A</u>. Assign each group one of the five mighty men from *2 Samuel 23* to research. Allow each group ten minutes to work on the sheet. Then, call the class back together

The Missing Chairs
15 Minutes

> **Materials You'll Need For This Session**
>
> Chalkboard, chalk, pens or pencils, Resource Sheets 12A and 12B, Transparency 12A

OPTION
Word Storm
8 Minutes

Most Valuable Mighty Man
30 Minutes

and give each group exactly two minutes (time them) to explain why their mighty man should be named the Most Valuable Mighty Man! After all the groups have finished, have the class vote for the Most Valuable Mighty Man. After the vote is complete, discuss with the class the question, **What qualities and actions made these particular men so noteworthy that we are still talking about them about 3,000 years after they died?** List insightful answers on the chalkboard.

OPTION
Class Discussion
25 Minutes

Pass out a copy of Resource Sheet 12B to each member of the class. Lead the class through a discussion of the questions, based on what we learn from *2 Samuel 23*. Encourage as much class participation as possible.

TAKING THE NEXT STEP

The Ultimate Mighty Man
15 Minutes

Display Transparency 12A. Work your way through Psalm 22, noting how Jesus' sacrifice on the cross indeed makes him the mightiest one of all for our lives. After sharing from Psalm 22, have the class break into prayer groups of four. Have the groups focus their prayers on thanking God for the sacrifice of Jesus on the cross and asking God for the strength to live lives of self-sacrifice.

OPTION
The Cost of Sacrifice
8 Minutes

Write the following two questions in large letters on the board: **For what or whom are you willing to sacrifice?** and **What specific sacrifices are you willing to make?** Divide the class into groups of two and have them discuss these questions. Have them close in prayer in their groups.

PLAN TWO roups

BUILDING COMMUNITY

1. Have the group discuss the question, **What makes a person truly great?**

2. OPTION: Have group members respond to these questions: **Who was your hero when you were ten years old? Why did you admire this person? Do you still respect this person today?**

CONSIDERING SCRIPTURE

Read 2 Samuel 23:8–23.

1. What is most impressive to you about the mighty men, the warriors who served David?

2. What was the key to the successes of the mighty men?

3. What specific sacrifices and risks were the mighty men willing to make for Israel, David, and the Lord?

4. Why do you think the mighty men were willing to take such risks?

5. How do you think the mighty men felt when David poured out the water they had risked their lives to get (vv. 13–17)?

6. In verse 39, we read that Uriah the Hittite, Bathsheba's husband, is listed among the mighty men of Israel. Does this surprise you? Why or why not?

7. Based on what we learn in this passage, would you say David was a successful leader? Why or why not?

8. Where do you think the mighty men learned to have such valor and commitment?

Accountability Partners
Have the partners respond to these questions: **What specific way can I serve others this coming week? What will I have to give up to do this?**

OPTION
Worship Ideas
Have the group read Psalm 22. Spend time praising God for the sacrifice of Jesus, the mightiest one of all. Also, pray that group members will learn to follow Jesus' example of self-sacrifice.

OPTION
Memory Verse
"All the ends of the earth will remember and turn to the Lord, and all the families of the nations will bow down before him" (Psalm 22:27).

TAKING THE NEXT STEP

1. For what or whom are you willing to sacrifice?

2. What specific sacrifices are you willing to make for the Lord?

Most Valuable Mighty Man

Which mighty man was the most mighty? Your task is to argue for one of the following candidates based on 2 Samuel 23. You will have two minutes to trumpet the cause of your candidate through moving and convicting oratory, so study your character and be creative. After all the groups have presented their candidates, the class will vote on a winner.

GROUP A: Josheb-Basshebeth (2 Samuel 23:8)

GROUP B: Eleazar son of Dodai (2 Samuel 23:9, 10)

GROUP C: Shammah son of Agee the Hararite (2 Samuel 23:11, 12)

GROUP D: Abishai son of Zeruiah (2 Samuel 23:18, 19)

GROUP E: Benaiah son of Jehoiada (2 Samuel 23:20, 23)

GROUP F: The Unknown Warriors (2 Samuel 23:13–17)

Class Discussion

Read 2 Samuel 23:8–23.

1. What is most impressive to you about the exploits of the mighty men?

2. What was the key to the successes of the mighty men?

3. What sacrifices were the mighty men willing to make for Israel, David, and the Lord?

4. Why do you think they were willing to make these sacrifices?

5. Based on this passage, do you think David was a successful leader? Why or why not?

6. Where do you think these mighty men learned to have such valor and commitment?

The Ultimate Mighty Man

Jesus is the mightiest man of all. Psalm 22 prophetically reveals the life of self-sacrifice he led for the sake of us all! The sacrifices of Jesus:

1. Forsaken by God
(Psalm 22:1; Matthew 27:46)

2. Insulted by the Mocking Crowd
(Psalm 22:6–8; Matthew 27:41–43)

3. Intense Pain and Overpowering Thirst
(Psalm 22:14, 15; John 19:28–30)

4. Hands and Feet Pierced by Evil Men
(Psalm 22:16; Luke 23:33; John 20:24–29)

5. Garments Divided and Treated as a Gambling Prize
(Psalm 22:18; Mark 15:24)

Thirteen

Famous Last Words

*I*n 2 Samuel 23, the Bible records the last words of King David. As David neared death, he was no longer a young, vigorous shepherd strong enough to fight lions, bears, and giants. Now he was a weary veteran, shivering in the cold no matter how many blankets his servants piled on him (1 Kings 1:1). . . .

David didn't deny the reality of death. He made sure his house was right with God. At the urging of his wife Bathsheba and his old friend Nathan the prophet, David made sure his son Solomon would succeed him as king (1 Kings 1:11–53). He gave Solomon some final instructions and charged him to be faithful to God (1 Kings 2:1–12). What kind of legacy will you leave to the next generation? Is your house right with God?

—David Faust, *Praise Under Pressure*

Central Theme   David's last words show how a child of God can face death with confidence and hope. When we come to the end of our lives, we'll be glad we offered God "praise under pressure."

Lesson Aim   Participants will explore their own attitudes and feelings about death and the hope Jesus provides, and will commit themselves to leave a legacy of faith to the next generation.

Bible Background   2 Samuel 23:1–7; 1 Kings 1 and 2; Psalm 103

For Further Study   Read Chapter 13 of *Praise Under Pressure*.

Classes

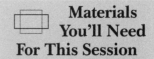 **Materials You'll Need For This Session**

Chalkboard and chalk, Resource Sheets 13A–C, Transparency 13A, pens or pencils

BUILDING COMMUNITY

Distribute copies of <u>Resource Sheet 13A</u>. This worksheet contains four biblical examples of encouraging words spoken by people near the end of their lives. Ask volunteers to read each of the quotations listed. Then ask everyone to fill in the section entitled "My Own Last Words." Say, **In three or four sentences, write what your own last words would be if today were to be your last day on earth.** Allow two or three minutes for participants to write their answers, and then ask a few volunteers to tell the rest of the class what they wrote.

Famous Last Words
8 Minutes

Before class begins, write the following statements on the chalkboard:
  1. "Most people don't think about death often enough or deeply enough."
  2. "You can learn more wisdom by going to a funeral home than by going to a party." (See Ecclesiastes 7:2.)
  Ask participants to raise their hands if they agree (or disagree) with each statement. Briefly discuss their answers.

OPTION
Agree-Disagree
8 Minutes

Write the word *death* on the chalkboard. Ask everyone to think silently and ponder their own feelings and beliefs about the idea of dying. After one minute of silence, ask all participants to find a partner and share their thoughts about death.

OPTION
Think/Pair/Share
5 Minutes

CONSIDERING SCRIPTURE

Lead into the Bible study by saying, **In 2 Samuel 23 and 1 Kings 1 and 2, the Bible tells us what King David was thinking and saying as he neared death. David's last words challenge us to explore our own attitudes and feelings about death, and to think about the legacy of faith we want to leave to the next generation when we die.**

Give everyone a copy of <u>Resource Sheet 13B</u>, "Through the Valley of the Shadow of Death." Divide the class into three small groups. Ask Group One to read 2 Samuel 23:1–7; Group Two to read 1 Kings 1:1–6, 28–37; and Group Three to read 1 Kings 2:1–12. Each group should select a leader to record

Small Group Discussion and Report
15–20 Minutes

their answers and serve as spokesperson. Each group will read the assigned Scripture text aloud, and then write several answers to the two questions listed on the resource sheet. After eight to ten minutes of discussion, ask each group to report its findings to the rest of the class.

Mini-Lecture
10 Minutes

Use <u>Transparency 13A</u> to highlight how David was able to face the end of his earthly life with confidence and hope. Emphasize a key verse, 2 Samuel 23:5, which reveals three important facts to consider as a believer approaches death. Use these quotes by David Faust from *Praise Under Pressure* to explain each point:

1. A House Right With God (2 Samuel 23:5: "Is not my house right with God?")

People say that time flies. If so, it doesn't float along like a hot air balloon. It speeds by like a rocket on supersonic wings. (See Psalm 103:15, 16; and James 4:14.) . . . . Our schedules can become so fast paced, there's little time to reflect on the significance and purpose of our lives. Maybe you've seen the Calvin and Hobbes cartoon that says, "God put me on this earth to accomplish a certain number of things, and right now I'm so far behind that I will never die." But we will die. . . . When Jerry Garcia died at the age of 53, fans and nonfans of his rock and roll music pondered the paradoxical name of his band, "The Grateful Dead." Grateful to die? Only if your house is right with God.

2. A Covenant Arranged by God (2 Samuel 23:5: "Has he not made with me an everlasting covenant, arranged and secured in every part?")

David faced death calmly because he trusted God's promises. . . . Years before, God made a special covenant (a solemn, binding agreement) to bless David and his descendants forever (2 Samuel 7:12–17). Despite all David's failures and faults, he relied on God's faithfulness. "But from everlasting to everlasting the Lord's love is with those who fear him, and his righteousness with their children's children—with those who keep his covenant and remember to obey his precepts" (Psalm 103:17, 18).

God is willing to enter into a covenant with us, too. It's not a covenant for only one person or one ethnic group, but for all people in every nation who accept the Lord. . . . It doesn't matter whether you're old or young, rich or poor. Your skin color doesn't matter, nor does the language you speak or even what you have done in the past. You can live forever in a covenant relationship with God! On the day you die, nothing will matter so much as this.

3. A Hope Guaranteed by God (2 Samuel 23:5: "Will he not bring to fruition my salvation and grant me my every desire?")

David's faith looked ahead with a glimmer of hope that spanned the centuries toward the one "who as to his human nature was a descendant of David, and who through the Spirit of holiness was declared with power to be the Son of God by his resurrection from the dead: Jesus Christ our Lord" (Romans 1:3, 4). . . .

Jesus isn't a fairy tale. Salvation isn't a religious pipe dream. Jesus' resurrection is a fact, not a myth. Empty hearts can find comfort in the Lord's empty tomb. He is alive! . . .

David . . . "died at a good old age, having enjoyed long life, wealth and honor" (1 Chronicles 29:28). But as David prepared to die, his greatest satisfaction came not from his possessions or the honors he received, but simply from the assurance that his life mattered to God.

TAKING THE NEXT STEP

Give everyone a copy of <u>Resource Sheet 13C</u>. Ask participants to write a sentence or two describing the spiritual legacy they want to leave to their family, to their church, and to their closest friends. Encourage a few volunteers to share their comments with the rest of the class. End the class by reading Psalm 103:19–22 and then closing in prayer.

Spiritual Last Will and Testament
10 Minutes

Groups

BUILDING COMMUNITY

1. What do you want on your tombstone?
Give everyone a note card and a pen or pencil. Ask participants to write a short epitaph they would like engraved on their tombstone when they die. These can be serious, thought-provoking, or humorous; but all should focus attention on the question, **How do you want people to remember you after you die?** After about two minutes, each person should show what she or he wrote on the note card.

2. OPTION: Give everyone a copy of <u>Resource Sheet 13A</u>. Ask participants to write what their own last words would be if today were their last day on earth. After about two minutes, each person should read what he or she wrote on the worksheet.

3. OPTION: Word Association: Let group members respond to the question, **What is the first thing that comes to mind when you hear the word** *death*?

CONSIDERING SCRIPTURE

Read 1 Kings 1:1–4.

1. This text paints a picture of David very different from that of his earlier years when he was a strong, vigorous shepherd who fought lions, bears, and giants. How do you think David felt about his declining strength?

2. How do you feel when you think about the physical problems or weaknesses you may experience with age?

Read 1 Kings 2:1–4.

3. What is the main point David is trying to pass on to his son Solomon?

4. Why is Solomon's obedience to God so important to David?

Read 2 Samuel 23:1–7.

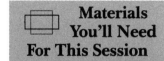
Materials You'll Need For This Session

Note cards, pens or pencils, Resource Sheets 13A and 13C

OPTION
Accountability Partners
Both partners should
write on a note card one
spiritual goal they want
to accomplish before
they die. Discuss and
pray over these goals,
and then exchange
cards. At a later time
(perhaps even a year or
two in the future), the
card can be mailed back
to the partner along with
a note encouraging her
or him to continue
pursuing the spiritual
goal written on the card.

OPTION
Worship Ideas
Open the group prayer
time by reading Psalm
103:1, 2. Ask group
members to find in
Psalm 103 at least one
reason they personally
want to praise God. For
example, "I praise God
because he doesn't treat
us as our sins deserve."
Conclude the prayer by
reading Psalm
103:19–22.

OPTION
Memory Verse
"Is not my house right
with God? Has he not
made with me an
everlasting covenant,
arranged and secured in
every part? Will he not
bring to fruition my
salvation and grant me
my every desire?"
(2 Samuel 23:5).

5. How would you describe David's frame of mind as he wrote these last words?
   a. **Satisfied with his accomplishments**
   b. **Bitter toward his enemies**
   c. **Secure in his own righteousness**
   d. **Insecure, and therefore trumpeting his own cause**
   e. **Secure in the Lord's grace and mercy**
   f. **Other:** _____

6. 2 Samuel 23:5 seems to be a key verse in understanding David's attitude as he approached death. Which of the following means the most to you as you think about your own death? Why?
   a. **"My house is right with God."**
   b. **"God has made an everlasting covenant with me."**
   c. **"God will bring to fruition my salvation and grant me my every desire."**
   d. **Other:** _____

Read Psalm 103:1–12.

7. As David reflected back on his life, what aspect of God's character seemed especially important to him? Given what we know about David's past failures, why do you think this quality of God was so significant for David as he neared death?

Read Psalm 103:13–18.

8. How can we really be filled with hope when life seems so short? (See also James 4:14; 2 Corinthians 4:16–18.)

9. How does the fact of Jesus' resurrection encourage you as you think about your own death? (See Romans 1:2–4; 1 Corinthians 15:3, 4; Hebrews 2:14, 15; 1 Peter 1:3.)

TAKING THE NEXT STEP

1. Give everyone a copy of Resource Sheet 13C. Ask participants to **write a few sentences describing the spiritual legacy you want to leave to your family, to your church, and to your closest friends.** After about three minutes, ask each person to share his or her comments with the rest of the group.

2. **Discuss what you have learned from studying the life of King David during the last several weeks. Overall, what are your lasting impressions of David? Has this study of *Praise Under Pressure* been helpful to you? How?**

Famous Last Words

EXAMPLES FROM SCRIPTURE

The Bible records many encouraging words spoken by faithful people near the end of their lives. For example . . .

MOSES: "The eternal God is your refuge, and underneath are the everlasting arms" (Deuteronomy 33:27).

JOSHUA: "Choose for yourselves this day whom you will serve. . . . But as for me and my household, we will serve the Lord" (Joshua 24:15).

STEPHEN: "Lord Jesus, receive my spirit" (Acts 7:59).

PAUL: "I have fought the good fight, I have finished the race, I have kept the faith" (2 Timothy 4:7).

MY OWN LAST WORDS

If today were to be *my* last day on earth, my last words would be:

Through the Valley of the Shadow of Death

GROUP ONE: 2 Samuel 23:1–7
GROUP TWO: 1 Kings 1:1–6, 28–37
GROUP THREE: 1 Kings 2:1–12

As David neared death, how would you describe his *attitude* or state of mind?

What *issues* or *concerns* seem most important to David as he faced death? Why?

My Spiritual "Last Will and Testament"

Write a sentence or two in each category below, describing the spiritual legacy you want to leave behind when you die.

To my **family**, I bequeath

To my **church**, I bequeath

To my **closest friends**, I bequeath

Facing Death With Confidence

2 Samuel 23:5

1. A House Right With God

(2 Samuel 23:5)

2. A Covenant Arranged by God

(2 Samuel 7:12–17; 23:5; Psalm 103:17, 18)

3. A Hope Guaranteed by God

(2 Samuel 23:5; 1 Thessalonians 4:13–18)

Other Creative Groups Guides
from Standard Publishing

THE NEW TESTAMENT CHURCH THEN AND NOW
13 complete lessons. Guide by Timothy Heck.
Learn how today's church can continue to carry out the same mission as the first-century church.
Order number 11-40322 *(ISBN 0-7847-0492-9)*

VICTORY IN JESUS
13 complete lessons. Guide by Jan Johnson.
Learn to live victoriously in your life in Christ.
Order number 11-40314 *(ISBN 0-7847-0424-4)*

FAITH'S FUNDAMENTALS
7 complete lessons. Guide by Kent C. Odor and Mark Ingmire.
Equip class and group members with the seven essentials of Christian belief.
Order number 11-40311 *(ISBN 0-7847-0391-4)*

DREAM INTRUDERS
6 complete lessons. Guide by Tim Sutherland.
Help group members learn to get through the difficult times and temporary setbacks in life.
Order number 11-40312 *(ISBN 0-7847-0392-2)*

FIND US FAITHFUL
13 complete lessons. Guide by Michael D. McCann.
Learn to pass on your faith to the next generation.
Order number 11-40308 *(ISBN 0-7847-0308-6)*

A CALL TO PRAYER
7 complete lessons. Guide by Jan Johnson.
Learn to pray more effectively, more sincerely, with more power, and without hindrances.
Order number 11-40309 *(ISBN 0-7847-0309-4)*

CLAIMING YOUR PLACE
7 complete lessons. Guide by Michael C. Mack and Mark A. Taylor.
Help your small group or class learn to find where they fit in the life of the church.
Order number 11-40305 *(ISBN 0-7847-0285-3)*

HEARING GOD
6 complete lessons. Guide by Michael C. Mack and Mark A. Taylor.
Help your group or class learn how to read God's Word—and really understand it!
Order number 11-40306 *(ISBN 0-7847-0286-1)*

To purchase a copy of

PRAISE UNDER PRESSURE,

contact your local
Christian bookstore.

(If the book is out of stock, you can order
by calling 1-800-543-1353.)
11-40319 *(ISBN 0-7847-0489-9)*